...eninsula,

ASIA

NORTH
PACIFIC
OCEAN

INDIAN OCEAN

AUSTRALIA

Best in Travel
Lonely Planet's

2015

The
Best in Travel
Promise

Where is the best place to visit right now?

As self-confessed travel geeks, our staff rack up hundreds of
thousands of miles each year, exploring most of the planet in
the process. And each year we ask everyone at Lonely Planet for
their latest recommendations – from our authors and editors to
our online family of bloggers and tweeters.

They come up with hundreds of places that are exciting
right now, offer new things for travellers to do, or are criminally
overlooked and underrated. Their list is whittled down by our
panel of travel experts to just 10 countries, 10 regions and 10
cities. Each is chosen for its topicality, unique experiences and
'wow' factor. We don't just report on the trends, we set them
– helping you get there before the crowds do.

Put simply, what remains in the pages that follow is the
cream of this year's travel picks, courtesy of Lonely Planet:
10 countries, 10 regions, 10 cities and a host of travel lists
to inspire you to explore for yourself.

So what are you waiting for?

12

54

Top 10
Countries

Top 10
Regions

96

Top 10
Cities

138

Top
Travel Lists

It's a special year for Lonely Planet's Best in Travel: we are 10 years old!

Top region 2014: Sikkim, India

The majestic profile of Mt Khangchendzonga looming over a sylvan mountainscape, magnificent red-and-gold Tibetan Buddhist monasteries, hearty platters of ethnic cuisine and close encounters with elusive red pandas and snow leopards – the list of attractions that repeatedly draw me to Sikkim is endless. ● *by Anirban Mahapatra, Lonely Planet India*

To celebrate, we're looking back over the last decade of travel inspiration from Lonely Planet, with a little help from our colleagues around the world – each of whom has followed hot tips featured in Best in Travel over the past 10 years to find out what all the fuss was about…

Top region 2013: Corsica

My 2013 road trip in Corsica was an amazing experience. I didn't know what to expect when I set out; what I found was a wonderful mix of nature and beaches. Bonifacio was maybe the most surprising, with its endless cliffs and caves. It's a place that has proved difficult to forget. ● *by Núria Puig, Lonely Planet Spain*

Top city 2012: London

I was pretty cynical about the London Olympics at first: it was going to cost the city a lot of money and wreak havoc with public transport. And yet somehow I ended up auditioning for, and performing in, the Opening Ceremony in a packed stadium in front of millions around the world. If that wasn't enough to dispel my cynicism then during the following weeks, during both the Olympics and Paralympics, I saw a side to London that I hadn't seen before. It was like the city was wearing a huge 'we did it, we actually did it' smile. It's a sense of pride and amazement that I am happy to say has outlasted the heady days of summer 2012. ● *by Clifton Wilkinson, Lonely Planet USA*

> "It was like the city was wearing a huge 'we did it, we actually did it' smile"

Top city 2011: New York

I went to New York in 2011 with my best friends. I liked the hectic Manhattan, but what I really loved was the cool vibe of Brooklyn, where you can enjoy a fresh lobster roll by the East River, hit the thrift shops of Williamsburg and spend a fun-filled beach day at Coney Island. ● *by Emeline Gontier, Lonely Planet France*

Top country 2010: El Salvador

That summer in El Salvador was surreal. From the Mayan pyramids in Tazumal I hitched a ride along the volcanic lakes and coffee farms of La Ruta de las Flores to a black-sand beach party in El Tunco. My friends poured in from the capital and over plates of pupusas we hatched plans for my favourite LP adventure. ● *by Tom Spurling, Lonely Planet author*

Top city 2009: Antwerp

Visiting Antwerp with my wife in 2009, it struck me that the city lacks the harmonious architectural style of its better-known Belgian siblings and, with its jarring mix of old and new, might easily be overlooked as an attractive city-break destination. But at its Central Station – the most beautiful I've ever seen – this cocktail of styles comes together beautifully, the retro glass and wrought-iron entrance contrasting with its futuristic multi-level platforms.

And the Sint Anna tunnel is another fascinating sight. The 500m-long gallery passes under the River Scheldt to emerge on the opposite bank, where you can admire the city from another spectacular viewpoint. ● *by Alberto Capano, Lonely Planet Italy*

Top region 2008: Glacier National Park, USA

Not all mountains are created equal. Glacier National Park is full of

stunning snow-filled peaks, lakes, waterfalls and wildlife that the Rocky Mountains easily gift to adventurous visitors. We marveled at the views from well-maintained but remote hikes. We worried over the receding glaciers. We camped under the stars. Put it all together and 'Glacier' brought a feeling of oneness with the earth that is difficult to find in normal day-to-day lives. ● *by Lou La Grange, Lonely Planet USA*

Top country 2007: Australia

In 2007 the book promised a Tasmania of wilderness combined with great food and excellent visitor facilities: as a nervous new parent with a taste for the outdoors, that sounded like the perfect combo.

Tassie more than delivered: miles of boardwalk across the wilds of Cradle Mountain were pushchair-friendly. Huge oysters were a dollar each, and we drank wine straight from the cellar-door. When we were caught in a summer snowstorm, we joined the pademelons, wombats and parakeets, and scuttled back to the comforts of our lair – a luxury wooden cabin. ● *by Piers Pickard, Lonely Planet UK*

Top country 2006: Croatia

The most memorable part of our time in Croatia was spent on the island of Mljet, one of the most southerly islands in the Dalmatia region. Our days on Mljet were focussed around the three crucial 'S's of life in coastal Croatia – seafood, swimming and sun! Our experience with food on Mljet was particularly unique when, through the course of a single day, we would snack on fresh bread delivered by the local baker (announcing his arrival with a toot of his horn on the street below our balcony), mussels literally hacked off the jetty by our waiter, and fish so fresh that we curiously watched our head-torch-wearing chef get into a boat, navigate a few 100m out into the water and pull up a net to select our main course. ● *by Georgina Leslie, Lonely Planet Australia*

Lonely Planet's Top Ten Countries

SINGAPORE'S HAWKER
STALLS ARE THE STUFF
OF LEGEND

Singapore

Grand heritage buildings, chaotic hawker centres, luxurious green spaces, glitzy shopping malls and a slew of new developments has elevated the 'Singapore experience' to new levels

EVENTS   FOOD   FAMILY

Population **5.4 million**
Foreign visitors per year **15.5 million**
Capital **Singapore**
Languages **English, Malay, Mandarin, Tamil**
Major industries **tourism, banking, biomedical sciences**
Unit of currency **Singapore dollar (S$)**
Cost index **plate of chicken rice or a bowl of laksa in a hawker centre from S$4 (US$3), artisan coffee from S$7 (US$5.50), hotel double/dorm from S$88/17.5 (US$70/14), standard MRT (metro) journey S$1.30 (US$1)**

1

Why go in 2015? > *Singapore turns 50*

As one of the world's most multicultural cities, Singapore is always celebrating something. But Asia's smallest state has an extra special reason to put on her party hat in 2015, for it's her Golden Jubilee.

Since sealing its independence in 1965, Singapore has been on a roll. And while its grand heritage buildings, chaotic hawker centres, luxurious green spaces and glitzy shopping malls have been luring travellers for decades, a slew of new developments has elevated the 'Singapore experience' to a whole new level.

Festivals & Events

Fancy floats, fire-breathing dragons and pyrotechnics collide at February's Chingay, Singapore's biggest street parade.

Have your wallets (and elbows) at the ready for the Great Singapore Sale, which sees retail prices slashed from the end of May until the beginning of July.

July's Singapore Food Festival provides ample opportunities to sample the city's top grub, and learn how to cook classic Malay, Chinese and Indian dishes yourself.

It's already Singapore's main event, but you can expect National Day, on 9 August, to be celebrated with ultra-extravagant fanfare in 2015.

First there's Marina Bay. From the now-iconic, boat-shaped Marina Bay Sands resort to otherworldly eco-park Gardens by the Bay, this new entertainment precinct is like a funfair for the whole family. And then there's the city's new crop of swanky hotels – between the W Singapore, Parkroyal on Pickering and the Sofitel So Singapore, it's difficult to keep track of the latest openings.

To coincide with the anniversary, Singapore is set to usher in a number of new attractions in 2015, including the National Art Gallery and the Singapore Sports Hub, which will host the 28th Southeast Asian Games. And with more than a dozen MRT (metro) extensions currently in development, it'll soon be easier to get around. Even Changi Airport, named the world's best at the 2014 Skytrax awards in Barcelona, will receive two new terminals (and a third runway) in the coming years.

CHINESE NEW YEAR LANTERNS ADD A SPLASH OF COLOUR AT MARINA BAY

Amid all this, Singapore has been nurturing an emerging local fashion scene, artisan coffee has taken off like wildfire, and brunch has become a 'thing'. While tucking into a plate of chilli crab at Lau Pa Sat will never go out of style, Singapore's fine dining scene is finally giving Bangkok, Hong Kong and Tokyo a run for their money, with two local restaurants making Asia's top 10 in San Pellegrino and Acqua Panna's 2014 list. And don't even get us started on Club St, the city's hottest new drinking and dining enclave

Combined, these elements make a pretty spectacular backdrop for a 50th birthday party. And given Singaporeans of all ages and creeds were invited to have a say in how the nation celebrates the landmark event as 'One People', it's sure to be a festive year ahead.

What's Hot...
Gardens by the Bay, hipster cafes, Sunday brunch at the Pan Pacific, Club St, Restaurant André, being green

---

What's Not...
The haze problem (created by Indonesia's controversial forest-burning for palm oil plantations), MRT breakdowns, Avalon (Marina Bay's mega-club closed its doors after just two years)

Life-changing experiences
Between its endless urban attractions and the serenity of its green spaces, arguably the most defining pleasure of Singapore is its food. Start your day with crispy, sweet kaya toast before allowing a local latte artist to create a masterpiece in a cup for you at one of the city's achingly hip new cafes. Head to a hawker centre to slurp down a spicy laksa lunch, being sure to leave room for dinner at one of Singapore's hottest celebrity restaurants.

Current craze
Singapore is firmly in the grip of the K-pop phenomenon. If you're not up with reality show *K-POP Star Hunt*, you'd be best not to admit it.

Random facts
■ Everyone who was present in Singapore on the date of independence was offered Singapore citizenship.
■ Singapore was declared the world's most expensive city in 2014, replacing Tokyo. The best things, after all, usually come at a price.
■ Singapore boasts some of the world's strictest laws with 'crimes' such as chewing gum and pornography (which includes answering the door in your underwear) carrying harsh penalties.

Most bizarre sight
Haw Par Villa. Set up by members of the Tiger Balm dynasty in the 1930s, this Chinese mythology-themed 'pleasure garden', complete with lurid depictions of hell, is one of the world's most bafflingly odd – not to mention gruesome – attractions. ● *By Sarah Reid*

GIRAFFES VISIT A WATERHOLE IN
NAMIBIA'S ETOSHA NATIONAL PARK

Namibia

Home to inspiring
landscapes, wildlife and
people, Namibia is now even
more rewarding thanks to
its progress in sustainable
development through
conservation and tourism

ADVENTURE · ACTIVITIES · OFF-ROAD

Population **2.2 million**
Foreign visitors per year **1.2 million**
Capital **Windhoek**
Languages **English (official),
Afrikaans, German, numerous
indigenous languages**
Major industry **mining (diamonds,
uranium, gold, base metals)**
Unit of currency **Namibian dollar (N$)**
Cost index **bottle of Windhoek Lager
N$6.50 (US$0.61), campsite per
person N$150 (US$14), safari lodge
double N$1000 (US$95), balloon
safari per person N$4000 (US$375)**

Why go in 2015? > Turning 25 and hitting its stride

The golden sands of Namibia turn silver this year
as the country is celebrating its 25th anniversary of
independence. And with memories of the country's birth still fresh in many
minds, expect the celebrations to be widespread and long lasting. There is
more for you to enjoy in 2015 than just a landmark birthday, though – the
country, home to inspiring desert and mountain landscapes, wildlife and
people, is now more rewarding than ever thanks to its ground-breaking
progress in sustainable development through conservation and tourism.

Already the first African country to include the protection of its environment within its constitution (one of a few in the world to do so), Namibia also empowers local and indigenous communities to contribute to conservation efforts and ensures that they receive an equitable distribution of the tourism proceeds relating to them. As a result, almost an eighth of Namibians are currently taking part, leading to registered conservancies covering more than 18% of the country's landmass. This, in addition to the 19% of Namibia that is protected as part of a national park or reserve, is playing a major role in the nation's conservation successes – it now hosts the world's largest numbers of black rhino and cheetah, and, unlike anywhere else on the continent, the populations and range of lions and giraffes are expanding.

With stories of poaching and habitat loss elsewhere in Africa dominating the news, word of Namibia's wildlife conservation successes hasn't yet gained too much traction. That won't last for long, however, so take advantage this year and explore it before you have to share it.

Life-changing experiences

Climb to the top of a sky-scraping red sand dune at Sossusvlei in the early hours and witness the day's first light seemingly set the desert landscape on fire. You'll need to stay within Namib-Naukluft National Park at either Sesriem Camp Site or Sossus Dune Lodge, the only two accommodations that allow pre-dawn access to the site.

Sleepless nights are a good thing. Well, in Etosha National Park anyway. Sit up into the wee hours at one of the park's three floodlit waterholes and be enthralled by the natural night-time theatrics of safari's big-name game.

Experience the sheer beauty and drama of the Skeleton Coast and its wildlife (both aquatic and terrestrial) on a low-altitude flight safari.

CONQUER THE MIGHTY DUNE AT NAMIB-NAUKLUFT NATIONAL PARK

Climb to the top of a sky-scraping red sand dune at Sossusvlei in the early hours and witness the day's first light seemingly set the desert landscape on fire

Festivals & Events

This year Namibia turns 25 on 21 March, so expect Independence Day to be rung in with grand style.

Musicians, dancers, poets and artists from many of Namibia's cultural groups are on show at Windhoek's /AE//Gams Art and Cultural Festival at the end of March.

In April the Capital erupts with live music, dancing and slapstick comedy at the Windhoek Karneval. In 2015, it kicks off with the Royal Ball on the 10th and finishes with the Kehraus (highlights show) on the 25th.

The Herero people of Okahandja commemorate Maherero Day (Heroes' Day) in late August with a procession through town. The vibrant traditional garb is a sight to see.

Current craze

Self-drive safaris. With evocative landscapes, empty roads and world-class wildlife, Namibia is simply the best place in Africa to get behind the wheel and explore. And with the western section of Etosha National Park recently opening up to self-drivers, there is more to see in 2015 than ever.

Trending topic

Oil. How will the development of recently discovered offshore deposits shape the country's coast and its economy?

Random facts

- Beetles, lizards, spiders and various plants in the depths of the Namib Desert collect their drinking water by ingeniously condensing fog on their extremities.
- The golden wheel spider escapes its predators in the desert by cartwheeling down dunes at a remarkable 2600 revolutions per minute.
- Although its remote shores are adorned with half-buried, bleached whale skeletons, the Skeleton Coast actually received its name due to its reputation for sinking ships, and the deadly environment that awaited the survivors.

Most bizarre sight

Kolmanskop, once a booming diamond-mining town complete with a hospital, school, church, theatre, bowling alley and casino – was deserted and left to be devoured by the Namib's shifting sands in the 1950s after richer deposits were found elsewhere. Today, Kolmanskop's dramatic half-digested remains are a surreal testament to the power of nature and to the wastefulness of disposable culture. ● *By Matt Phillips*

SOAK UP THE
ATMOSPHERE IN
VILNIUS' OLD TOWN

Lithuania

There'll be plenty of fanfare and public events to mark the occasion of the last Baltic nation joining the European common currency

CULTURE · ACTIVITIES · VALUE

Population **3 million**
Foreign visitors per year **985,700**
Capital **Vilnius**
Languages **Lithuanian, Russian**
Major industry **manufacturing**
Unit of currency **litas (Lt); euro (€) in 2015**
Cost index **bottle of Švyturys beer 8 Lt (US$3.20), sit-down meal per person 20–40 Lt (US$8–16), double hotel room 150–300 Lt (US$60–120)**

3

Why go in 2015? > Euros à gogo on the Baltic!

Well, as of 1 January 2015, Lithuania will be one of the family... well, the Euro family at least. As the newest member of the eurozone, Lithuania will take the final step in its journey from east to west, from reluctant Soviet republic to fully fledged European nation. When the 35 artists who launched the Reform Movement of Lithuania began their quest for independence from the Soviet Union in 1990, who knew how far it would go?

From a visitor perspective, this means travelling in Lithuania is going to get a whole lot easier, particularly when it comes to electronic payments and finding an ATM. However, it may not get cheaper – the rate of exchange for the switchover is still to be decided and some 55% of Lithuanians are nervous about what the change means for the litas in their pocket. What is guaranteed is lots of fanfare and public events to mark the occasion of the last Baltic nation joining the European common currency.

Life-changing experiences

The seaside probably isn't the first thing that springs to mind when people think of Lithuania, but the Curonian Spit is one long line of gorgeous beaches stretching south towards Russia, backed by Europe's largest moving sand dunes. This wasn't always sand and marram grass – the spit was once densely forested, before the trees were felled to build boats for the Battle of Gross-Jägersdorf (1757). Today, the spit is World Heritage listed, and the most popular holiday spot in the country – to help keep it beautiful, free tickets are offered to visitors who carry 120L of rubbish away when they leave.

Then there's lovely Vilnius, whose baroque old town – the largest in northern Europe – earned Lithuania its second entry on the World Heritage list. Like a less cutesy and less commercial Prague, the old quarter is a warren of winding alleyways and cobbled squares flanked by curlicue-covered town-houses. Teutonic statues and occasional onion domes lend a definite Russian flavour, but there's refreshingly little pressure to buy a furry *ushanka* hat.

↑

What's Hot...
Eurobasket, the Eurovision Song Contest, standing up to Russia, particularly after events in Crimea

—

What's Not...
Any mention of rejoining Russia, particularly after events in Crimea

↓

Current craze

Love for shooting hoops runs deep in Lithuania, where basketball tournaments between Lithuanian and Soviet teams became an allegory for the greater struggles of the Cold War. 'Eurobasket' is consistently the most popular word entered into Lithuanian online search engines and ten former Lithuanian players have made it to the American NBA. The above-average height of Lithuanians – nearly 4cm taller than the European norm – may well have played a part.

Siauliai's Hill of Crosses is a weather-worn collection of around 100,000 crucifixes of every imaginable kind and size

THE EERIE HILL OF CROSSES IS A POWERFUL SIGHT TO BEHOLD

Random facts

- Mindaugas, who united Lithuania in the 13th century, was the country's first and only monarch.
- Lithuania was the first Soviet Republic to declare independence, leading the charge in 1990.
- Vilnius proudly displays the world's only statue to Frank Zappa, replacing a Communist monument that was torn down after Independence.

Most bizarre sights

Topping the list of unlikely attractions is Grūto Parkas, popularly known as Stalin World, with its statues of 'heroic workers' and rescued busts of Lenin and Uncle Joe, spread around a forest park guarded by gulag-style watchtowers. The theme park's founder, mushroom-mogul Viliumas Malinauskas, insists that the park exists to make fun of Communism, but plans for Siberian-style 'deportation' trains to ferry tourists from Vilnius were flatly rejected by local officials!

Almost as strange is Siauliai's Hill of Crosses, a weather-worn collection of around 100,000 crucifixes of every imaginable kind and size, groaning under the weight of rosaries and devotional offerings. The first crosses appeared here after the 1831 uprising against Russian rule, and the collection is still growing (new additions are positively encouraged).

- *By Joe Bindloss*

Festivals & Events

Actually ten festivals in one, the Vilnius Festival showcases everything from classical music and jazz to dance, theatre and cinema during the month of June.

Klaipėda, Lithuania's only seaport, gets in the nautical mood in July for the annual Sea Festival, with regattas, live music and a huge craft fair.

In August, the beachside village of Karklė rocks out for three days for the unimaginatively named but thoroughly entertaining Karklė Live Music Beach Festival.

THE YELLOW CATEDRAL DE GRANADA
DOMINATES THE SKYLINE OF NICARAGUA'S
MOST FAMOUS COLONIAL CITY

Nicaragua

Explore Nicaragua's quaint colonial (albeit bullet-holed) towns, riotous folkloric fiestas and enchantingly undeveloped Caribbean islands

ADVENTURE | VALUE | ACTIVITIES

Population **6.1 million**
Foreign visitors per year **1 million**
Capital **Managua**
Language **Spanish (and English on Atlantic Coast/Islands)**
Major industries **agriculture, tourism**
Unit of currency **córdoba (C$)**
Cost index **hotel double/dorm from C$1000/260 (US$40/10), short taxi ride C$80 (US$3), bottle of Toña beer C$25 (US$1), street-vendor nacatamal (savoury, steamed corn meal snack) C$20 (US$0.80)**

Why go in 2015? › Livin' Latino-luxe

Nica neophytes have long been touting Nicaragua as 'the new Costa Rica'. And in the sense that it's cheaper, safer and less developed than its Central American neighbour, we can see why. But ask any local, and they'll tell you that far from any imitation, Nicaragua is a unique natural playground with a history, culture and cuisine all of its own.

Nothing attracts backpackers like a bargain, and intrepid adventure-seekers have secretly been flocking to mainland Latin America's poorest country to surf San Juan del Sur's blissfully uncrowded breaks, 'board' down an active volcano near *León*, and hike through the cloud forests of Isla de Ometepe, for

What's Hot...
The Emerald Coast, Little Corn Island, eco-lodges, the quesillos (street snack)-per-córdoba ratio, sunset macuás (the national cocktail) mixed with gold-label Flor de Caña (the national rum)

What's Not...
Referring to the United States as 'America' (Nicaraguans consider themselves Americans, too), divulging the nation's still-secret surf spots, the Nicaragua Canal project, catching taxis in Managua

↓

years. But despite the added draws of Nicaragua's quaint colonial (albeit bullet-holed) towns, riotous folkloric fiestas and enchantingly undeveloped Caribbean islands, the stigma of its war-torn past has traditionally kept the wider travel community at bay.

Then came Mukul. The nation's first fully fledged five-star resort threw open its doors to international applause in 2013, closely followed by laid-back-luxe Yemaya Island Hideaway and Spa over on Little Corn Island. As if on cue, the UN then declared Nicaragua the second-safest Latin country, and suddenly a romantic jaunt down to this exotic little corner of the world started to sound like a pretty good idea to everyone. It has now garnered a

name for itself as one of the world's top emerging luxury ecotourism destinations, and foodies have been raving about the new crop of stylish restaurants that have morphed Managua, a former no-go zone, into a fledgling culinary capital.

But while Nicaragua has, for the most part, been busy painting itself a bright green future, a controversial new plan designed to boost its still-flagging economy threatens to put it back in the red. With a giant shipping canal – to rival neighbouring Panama's – set to be cut through the bowels of the country, there's no better time to enjoy Nicaragua in its natural (and cheap!) splendour than at this very moment.

Life-changing experiences
Its status as the birthplace of volcano boarding is the first hint that Nicaragua is an adventurist's dream. Try your luck at beating the km/hr record flying down steaming Cerro Negro on a custom-

Its status as the birthplace of volcano boarding is the first hint that Nicaragua is an adventurist's dream

FOR THE ULTIMATE ADRENALINE KICK, TRY VOLCANO BOARDING DOWN NICARAGUA'S CERRO NEGRO

Festivals & Events

Granada's International Poetry Festival (February) attracts rhymsters from all corners of the globe. There are also concerts by some of Nicaragua's best musicians.

On Nicaragua's Day of the Revolution (19 July), you'll understand just how much the people love President Daniel Ortega when you see the master work a crowd of 100,000 red-and-black-flag-waving faithful in the capital.

built sled near *León*, Central America's oldest city, or strap on your hiking boots and attempt the summit of Isla de Ometepe's majestic Volcan Mederas. A largely untapped surfing destination, Nicaragua also boasts one of the world's few remaining coastlines where you can routinely get the lineups all to yourself – if you're willing to sniff them out. As for the diving, the barrier reef system fringing the Corn Islands is one of the Caribbean's most pristine.

Officially it's eight days of festivities starting in late September, but the usually sleepy town of Masaya stretches out the feast of San Jerónimo, Nicaragua's most famous fiesta, to three months. Fireworks, marimbas, parades, drag queens and more make it one to remember.

Current craze

Celebrity golfers have been clamouring to tee off at the David McLay Kidd–designed course at luxury Emerald Coast resort Mukul since *Forbes* named it one of the world's 'top five great new golf resorts you need to know'.

Trending topic

Clearing an estimated 400,000 hectares of rainforest and wetland to build Nicaragua's answer to the Panama Canal has enraged environmentalists, who argue the project will threaten fresh water supplies, cut off wildlife migration routes and further endanger the country's rare species.

Most bizarre sight

Rolling into *León*, it's difficult to miss the hordes of elated, ash-covered travellers enjoying post-volcano-boarding mojitos at Bigfoot Hostel. Its former Australian owner is credited with founding the sport a decade ago and you'd be mad to leave town without trying it. ● *By Sarah Reid*

A BREATHTAKING VIEW FROM
VALENTIA ISLAND TO IVERAGH
PENINSULA IN COUNTY KERRY

Ireland

This year is the year of the Wild Atlantic Way, a 1500km scenic drive being sold as a rival to California's Pacific Coast Highway and Australia's Great Ocean Road

CULTURE	EVENTS	ACTIVITIES

Population **6.4 million (4.59 million in the Republic, 1.81 million in Northern Ireland)**

Foreign visitors per year **7.5 million**

Capital **Dublin**

Languages **English, Irish**

Major industry **exports, mainly textiles, machinery and food items**

Unit of currency **euro (€)**

Cost index **pint of Guinness €5–6 (US$6.90–8.27), midrange hotel double €60–120 (US$83–165), daily midsize car rental €45 (US$62), round of golf at a top course €80–150 (US$110–206)**

→ **Why go in 2015?** > *Separating blarney from bunkum*

You know the songs – hell, you probably sang some of them after drinking a few beers and declaring yourself part-Irish on 17 March. Ireland is small, but it packs a big punch, thanks to those millions of emigrants who left to earn a crust so they wouldn't have to subsist on one.

Absence makes the heart grow fonder, and when that absence stretches across the generations, well... there's a whole lot of love for the old country. Which carries with it a burden of expectation, invariably skewed towards the sheep-on-the-road, thatched-roof-on the cottage variety. An image that is slightly at odds with the modern Ireland of motorways and macchiatos that the Irish themselves have worked hard to develop. There aren't that many folk songs about broadband speed on the Aran Islands, but there's plenty of debate about it.

But the Irish know which side their tourist bread is buttered and it's all about scenery, tradition and the warm welcome – 100,000 of them, if you believe the spiel. Beneath the touristic tomfoolery, though, is the real deal: Ireland is stunningly scenic, its traditions – music, dance, whiskey and beer – firmly intact and the cosmopolitan, contemporary Irish are just as friendly and welcoming as their forebears were known to be.

This year is the year of the Wild Atlantic Way, a 1500km scenic drive that is being sold as a rival to California's Pacific Coast Highway and Australia's Great Ocean Road. It snakes its way round every nook and crook of the western seaboard from Donegal to Cork – start your journey with a feast of crab claws in Inishowen and reward your endeavours with some smoked salmon in Kinsale. Along the way, explore Connemara, the Aran Islands, the music bars of County Clare and the scenic splendours of County Kerry. Go west.

Life-changing experiences

The Irish themselves are inevitably at the heart of the best the country has to offer. Attend a traditional music session in a small pub in

Festivals & Events

March 17 – St Patrick's Day – is now such a big deal that it's become St Patrick's Festival and it's spread over three or four days. Fireworks, gigs and parades for the kids, a long day's 'celebrating' for the adults.

Summertime in Galway is festival madness – kicking off in July with the Galway Arts Festival, following on with the film festival and race week in August and the oyster festival in September.

All-Ireland Finals: the second and fourth Sundays of September are the biggest sporting days of the year, as the finals of the Gaelic football and hurling championships take place at Croke Park stadium in Dublin.

To keep the winter blues at bay, catch the best of the country's traditional music and dance at the Ennis Trad Festival, five days of sessions, master classes, CD launches and a *céilí* (party), held in November in Ennis, County Clare.

> **The Irish themselves are inevitably at the heart of the best the country has to offer**

County Clare. Hook up with a walking club and do a little cross-country ambling on a soft Sunday afternoon. Go surfing at Rossnowlagh Beach in County Donegal. Or just strike up a conversation over a pint with the gang sitting next to you in the pub. It's these connections that will make you want to come back.

Trending topic

The economy, stupid. And holding those who ruined it to account. The global financial crisis decimated the Irish economy, forcing it into an onerous bailout program It only exited last year. As the country reels from five years of body blows, it's trying to figure out why, how and, especially, who.

Random facts

- Halloween comes from the Irish harvest festival called Samhain.
- America's White House was designed by Irish architect James Hoban, who drew inspiration from Leinster House in Dublin, now the Irish Parliament.
- The expression 'by hook or by crook', as in 'by any means necessary', refers to Oliver Cromwell's attempts to capture Waterford in the 17th century, by Hook Head or the village of Crook.

Most bizarre sight

A goat is crowned king and everybody drinks for three days – it's just another edition of August's Puck Fair in Killorglin, County Kerry – Ireland's quirkiest festival. ● *By Fionn Davenport*

LEARN TO SURF ON ROSSNOWLAGH BEACH IN DONEGAL BAY: A BRACING WAY TO ENCOUNTER THE NORTH ATLANTIC WATERS

AN ENCOUNTER WITH CONGO'S
WESTERN LOWLAND GORILLA CAN
BE A HUMBLING EXPERIENCE

Republic of Congo

For those ready to heed the call of the wild, and not afraid of real, genuine adventure, the Congo awaits

ADVENTURE | ACTIVITIES | CULTURE

Population **4.3 million**

Foreign visitors per year **85,000**

Population of western lowland gorillas **around 125,000**

Capital **Brazzaville**

Languages **French, Lingala, Munukutuba**

Major industries **oil, timber**

Unit of currency **Central African franc (CFA)**

Cost index **gorilla trekking permit CFA190,000 (US$400), seven-hour bus ride CFA19,000 (US$40), budget hotel room CFA10,000–16,600 (US$20–35)**

6

↳ **Why go in 2015?** > Go ape for the jungles of the Congo

The Congo. Few words conjure up such images of exotica: sweltering jungles populated by chest-thumping gorillas, paddle-wheel steamers sailing down mud-brown rivers a mile wide, pygmies dancing in honour of forest spirits, masses of elephants and hooting, swinging troops of chimpanzees. The Congo (not to be confused with the neighbouring, and far more unpredictable, Democratic Republic of Congo) stands on the cusp of a new era. It's got oil, it's got timber, it's got a rapidly expanding infrastructure and after many turbulent years it's finally safe and stable. But more than anything else the Congo, with its stash of national parks and other protected areas covering enormous swathes of barely touched rainforest filled with the calls of great apes and lumbering elephants, has the potential to become one of Africa's finest ecotourism destinations. Right now foreign tourists are as rare as an albino gorilla, but the Congolese government, looking at the money generated by safari-royalty nations such as Kenya and Tanzania, is keen to change that and knows that it's the nations apes and elephants (albino or not) that will bring in the punters. And so, over the past few years, it has set to work rehabilitating old national parks, establishing new ones and updating the tourism infrastructure.

This revamping culminated in the recent opening by Wilderness Safaris of two upmarket safari lodges deep in the gorilla-infested forests of Parc National d'Odzala. With their unveiling, those of us with an inner Tarzan can now paddle pirogues down backwater rivers and come face to face with Congolese megafauna in relative ease and comfort.

So, for those ready to heed the call of the wild, and not afraid of real, genuine adventure, the Congo awaits.

ROAD IMPROVEMENTS ARE UNDERWAY THROUGHOUT THE CONGO, MAKING IT EASIER THAN EVER TO EXPLORE ITS WILDERNESSES

Life-changing experience

Being led by a barefoot BaAka (pygmy) guide through a Congolese swamp for an up-close-and-personal encounter with a rough-and-tumble family of western lowland gorillas is an experience that can be both humbling and inspiring – or, when a big male silverback comes crashing through the forest towards you, just plain old terrifying.

Current craze

Roads. Most of us take them for granted, but for as long as anyone can remember a road in the Congo generally meant a large, muddy pothole. Today work crews are busy up and down the country laying down tarmac and opening up areas that have been almost inaccessible for, well, forever really.

Trending topics

Making headlines around the world (but sadly not appearing to make much difference), the surging demand for ivory products in parts of Asia is fuelling a poaching epidemic that's decimating elephant populations across Africa. The hardest hit areas are the lightly policed and often poorly protected forests of Central Africa and some experts believe that at current rates forest elephants could be extinct in Central Africa within a decade.

Festivals & Events

The Congo doesn't go in for big crowd pleasing festivals and events. Local village festivals celebrating marriages, circumcisions, deaths and births are the most common, as are those performed by the BaAka and others in honour of forest spirits. By their nature these are always spontaneous affairs and you'd be lucky to witness one. Of the nationwide events the biggest is National Day Congo on 15 August when military parades in Brazzaville and other towns mark the anniversary of independence from France.

Most bizarre sight

In the far north of Congo, and surrounded by almost totally unexplored and unmapped swamp forest, is the near perfectly circular Lac Télé (Lake Télé). This is one of the remotest corners of Africa and it's thought the forests around the lake are home to an estimated 100,000 lowland gorillas as well as masses of chimpanzees, forest elephants and buffalo, as well as BaAka groups living an almost totally traditional lifestyle. But according to the local BaAka, Lac Télé is also home to something even more formidable than a gorilla: the legendary *mokélé-mbèmbé*, a large semi-aquatic creature that is described as being similar to a sauropod, a type of long extinct dinosaur.

● *By Stuart Butler*

Those of us with an inner Tarzan can paddle pirogues down backwater rivers and come face to face with Congolese megafauna

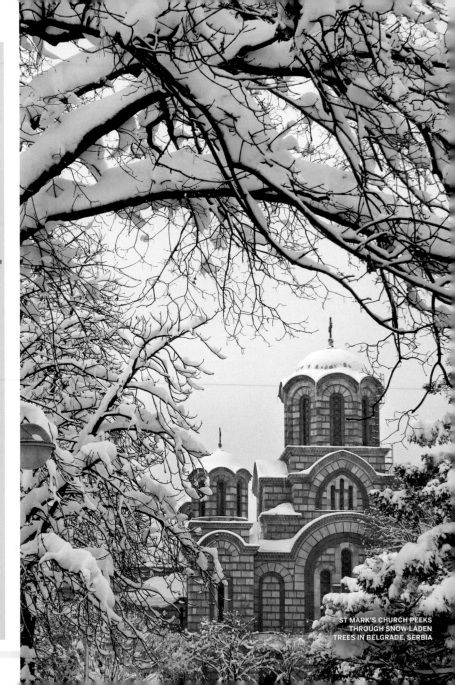

ST MARK'S CHURCH PEEKS
THROUGH SNOW-LADEN
TREES IN BELGRADE, SERBIA

Serbia

For partying, passion and personality, this small – and for now, astonishingly inexpensive – country is one of Europe's best-kept secrets

EVENTS | CULTURE | OFF ROAD

Population **7.2 million**
Foreign visitors per year **921,800**
Capital **Belgrade**
Language **Serbian**
Major industries **services and agriculture (the world's largest raspberry exporter)**
Unit of currency **Serbian dinar (RSD)**
Cost index **dorm room for a night 1140 RSD (US$13.60), litre of homemade *rakija* 500 RSD (US$6), *trubači* serenade, one song 300 RSD (US$3.60), one-day main season ski ticket 3550 RSD (US$42)**

7

Why go in 2015? > Get in while the gettin's good

Balkan backpacker buses bypass it in favour of 'easier' neighbours like Croatia and Bulgaria. The loss of erstwhile nation-partner Montenegro means it has no coastline. People regularly confuse it with Siberia. It's the birthplace of modern tennis legends, but nobody can pronounce their names. And then there's the small matter of Serbia being a former international pariah. But for partying, passion and personality, this small – and for now, astonishingly inexpensive – country is one of Europe's best-kept secrets.

You'll have to get in quick, though: Serbia is already making headlines for the right reasons. The genre-jumping Exit Festival – annexing a medieval fortress in Novi Sad each July since it began 15 years ago as an anti-Slobodan Milošević protest in 2000 – was recently awarded the Best Major European Festival title; Belgrade, with its hedonistic floating nightclubs, is being mentioned in the same panting breaths as Berlin and Ibiza; and Serbia's al fresco amusements – killer skiing in Kopaonik, spa-hopping in Vrnjačka Banja, rafting the Drina River, all of them cheap, cheap, cheap – are luring thrillseekers away from pricey, played-out playgrounds in 'the other Europe'.

One secret that hasn't yet been spilled? The Serbs themselves. While famous natives – think Palme d'Or-winning director Emir Kusturica, controversial performance artist Marina Abramovic and a certain Novak Djokovic – steal the spotlight, it's the everyday Serbs that may prove to be the country's greatest drawcard. Forthright, fun-loving and all too ready to welcome visitors with a hearty backslap and a glass of *rakija* (fiery local moonshine), they're more than the stereotypical scoundrels Hollywood would have us believe.

But in 2015 Serbia is edging towards EU ascension, meaning big changes – and big crowds – are coming. Go. Now. Before the *rakija* runs out.

Life-changing experiences

Listen out for the loudest place on the street, any street, anywhere.

> **The genre-jumping Exit Festival was recently awarded the Best Major European Festival title**

Festivals & Events

July's Exit Festival rocks Novi Sad's Petrovaradin Fortress to its sturdy foundations: 200,000 revellers, a truckload of awards and a million missing brain cells can't be wrong. 2015 marks 15 years since its inception: it's gonna be a big one.

August is HUGE. Belgrade staggers through its four-day Beerfest; the city of Niš gets its jazz hands on for Nišville; and the daddy of them all, the Guča Trumpet Festival, is a four-day bacchanalia of booze and brass: thousands of gypsy trumpeters will blast you into bedlam... in the best possible way.

Go inside. This is *kafana*, somewhat akin to a pub or taverna, but with more shouting and smoke. You'll see Serbs engaging in their national pastime (arguing), mayhap a smashed bottle or two (don't fret: this is merely punctuation) and if you're lucky, be serenaded by a ramshackle *trubači* (trumpet) band who will mistake your eardrum for a microphone. Don't walk past: *kafana* IS Serbia.

Head to the hills for a (literally) dyed-in-the-wool village experience. Mokra Gora is a sleepy, sheepy hamlet in Serbia's west, but there's more to do here than chew your cud: ride the Šargan 8 steam train through precarious, preternatural mountain passes; explore Drvengrad, the whimsical village-within-a-village built by director

Emir Kusturica for indie classic *Life is a Miracle*; and try to walk without wobbling after a *rakija* and *roštilj* (barbecue) session with obliging locals.

Go boho in Belgrade's own mini-Montmartre. The quaint, cobblestoned streets of Skadarlija are lined with raucous inns, offbeat galleries and meandering musicians redolent of the quarter's heyday as a haven for artistes, gypsies and olde-timey hipsters.

Serbia isn't the quietest place on the planet, but you can find a bit of shush in any of the country's medieval monasteries. Fruška Gora is home to the highest concentration of the Orthodox cloisters, 16 of them all tucked up tight in a 50km-long stretch of sylvan hills and ancient vineyards.

Depleted after the August debauch? Head south to Leskovac for September's Roštiljijada (barbecue festival) and chow your way through this year's attempts at the world's biggest *pljeskavica* (Serbian hamburger): a previous entry weighed in at 51kg.

Most bizarre sight

Đavolja Varoš (Devil's Town) is a trippy cluster of 202 natural stone pyramids looming eerily over bright red, highly acidic mineral streams. According to local whispers, the towers – which teeter between 2 and 15m high and are topped with creepy volcanic 'heads' – were formed after guests at an incestuous wedding were petrified by an offended god. ● *By Tamara Sheward*

A SANDY SUN-DRENCHED
PARADISE AWAITS ON PANDAN
ISLAND IN PALAWAN

The Philippines

It's officially Visit Philippines Year, and if there's one thing Filipinos know how to do, it's throw a party - expect street parades, food festivals, sports tournaments and live music shows

ACTIVITIES

ADVENTURE

OFF ROAD

Population **99 million**

Foreign visitors per year **4.6 million**

Capital **Manila**

Language **Filipino (Tagalog)**

Major industry **agriculture**

Unit of currency **peso (₱)**

Cost index **bottle of San Miguel beer ₱50 (US$1.15), double hotel room ₱1000–2000 (US$22–44), one-tank dive ₱1500–1800 (US$33.50–40.20)**

Why go in 2015?
> *Could this be the Philippines' breakthrough year?*

Many would say the time is well overdue for the Philippines to be recognised as the next big travel destination in Southeast Asia. With more than 7100 islands (compare that to Thailand, with a paltry 1430), the Philippines has one of the world's most beautiful coastlines, fringed by dive-tastic coral reefs, sprinkled with sunbathe-ready white sand, backed by swaying palm trees and dotted with simple resorts of *nipa*-palm thatched huts, like Thailand used to be when the Beach Boys were still top of the charts.

Officially, 2015 is Visit Philippines Year, and the government is laying on all

A LARGER-THAN-LIFE JEEPNEY IN SANTA CRUZ AWAITS ITS PASSENGERS

What's Hot...

Peace, thanks to the signing of a historic treaty between the Philippines government and the unfortunately abbreviated MILF, the Moro Islamic Liberation Front

What's Not...

Climate change: 2013 saw one of the worst typhoon seasons in living memory, culminating in the devastation of Typhoon Haiyan

sorts of special events to raise the profile of the archipelago. And if there's one thing Filipinos know how to do, it's throw a party – expect street parades, food festivals, sports tournaments and live music shows, with lavish sponsorship from powerhouse brands like San Miguel and Beer Na Beer. In fact, thanks to the Filipino love of live music, a cabaret atmosphere prevails almost every night. Now that Philippine Airlines has gained approval for direct flights to Europe, America and Australia, what are you waiting for?

Life-changing experience

There are plenty! Try clinging to the back of a jeepney speeding through the crowded streets of Metro Manila. Based on US Army jeeps left behind after WWII, these stretched wonders are part public bus and part art installation, adorned with extravagant chrome trim, custom upholstery, hundreds of decals and dozens of superfluous lights. Boarding and disembarking from these supercharged vehicles is conducted at break-neck speed, then it's back into the traffic, horn blaring, music blasting, and on to the next stop.

Current craze

Gosh, what isn't a craze in the Philippines? Filipinos love fads, and everything from the yoyo to the sellotape selfie (yep, that's a portrait of your own face bound up with sellotape) has had its moment in the sun in the Philippines. Indeed, the city of Makati was recently feted as the world's 'selfiest' city. One craze that never goes out of fashion in the Philippines is karaoke – alone, or in company, Pinoys love to sing, and no social gathering or business meeting would be complete without a swift rendition of the latest hits on the karaoke machine.

Trending topic

Flesh-eating bacteria and apocalyptic prophecies, apparently. In 2011, a news story about a new skin disease in Pangasinan province sparked a social media panic, as locals linked the outbreak to an end-of-the-world prophecy made by an Indian holy man. Within hours, the hashtag #PrayForPangasinan had been tweeted by more than 80,000 people. While officially Catholic, many Filipinos are extremely superstitious, embracing everything from faith healers to *kulam* (old-fashioned witchcraft).

Random facts

■ The colours of the Philippines flag are officially reversed in wartime – if you see a red band on the top of the flag, beware...
■ The modern yoyo was invented by a Filipino – the word 'yoyo' means 'come back' in Tagalog.
■ 1.39 billion SMS messages are sent every day in the Philippines.

Most bizarre sight

Live crucifixion. But don't worry, the devout Christians who offer themselves up for real, but temporary, crucifixion in San Fernando de Pampanga every Good Friday do so on a strictly voluntary basis. Regarded as the ultimate sign of religious devotion, this gruesome practice can be habit-forming – former construction worker Ruben Enaje has been crucified every year since 1985!

● *By Joe Bindloss*

Festivals & Events

Indigenous costumes with extravagant modern embellishments take centre-stage at the Ati-Atihan Festival in Kalibo, Aklan, from 17 to 19 January.

On the last Sunday of January, Iloilo City goes crazy for the Dinagyang Festival, with pulsing street parades and some of the most outrageous floats this side of Mardi Gras.

Every Holy Week (29 March to 4 April in 2015), locals dressed as Roman centurions scour the island of Marinduque in search of Longinus, the soldier who pierced the side of Christ, as part of the Moriones festival.

These stretched wonders are adorned with extravagant chrome trim, custom upholstery, hundreds of decals and dozens of superfluous lights

THE FISHING TOWN OF CANARIES
IN ST LUCIA NESTLES ON THE
WINDING WEST COAST ROAD

St Lucia

Take advantage of what everyone else isn't doing and make 2015 the year you visit St Lucia. There's no way a place this charming can stay secret for long

ACTIVITIES | ADVENTURE | OFF-ROAD

Population **673,000**
Foreign visitors per year **350,000**
Capital **Castries**
Languages **English, St Lucian Creole French**
Major industries **tourism, bananas**
Unit of currency **East Caribbean dollar ($)**
Cost index **beer in beachfront bar EC$5 (US$1.90), double room at boutique resort in high season EC$662 (US$245), minibus fare EC$1.50 (US$0.60), single tank dive EC$105 (US$40)**

9

Why go in 2015?
> *Visit this little island paradise before it hits the big time*

This ravishing island of emerald mountains and golden beaches sings its siren song year-round. Its main city of Castries is loaded with shopping, dining and sightseeing opps. And with primo diving and snorkelling, hikeable rainforests, and even a drive-in volcano (yeah, you heard us), it's also got all the right stuff for the off-the-beaten-path adventurer.

When it comes to nature, St Lucia thrills. Swim in the blood-warm waters alongside dolphins, take out a pair of binoculars and try to spot the island's unique species of parrot, catch sea turtles laying eggs on Grand Anse beach, or observe an iguana sunning itself on a log. Those seeking solitude can explore the secluded villages of the interior or the quiet sandy coves of the east coast. Thrill-seekers should climb the Piton mountains, kite surf Sandy Beach, or dive magnificent coral-crusted undersea walls.

But despite its splendour, this remote island paradise is still little-visited except for the usual cruise-ship traffic and in-the-know French couples. Take advantage of what everyone else isn't doing and make 2015 the year you visit St Lucia. There's no way a place this charming can stay secret for long.

Life-changing experiences

Glide through the treetops in the heart of the St Lucia rainforest on a zip-line tour with Rain Forest Adventure. If you're an adrenaline junkie who finds walking nature tours a bit… pedestrian, this is the activity for you. Take in the sights, sounds and smells of the tropical forest – prehistoric-looking ferns, buzzing insects, voluptuous jungle flowers – from a bird's perspective. For the less Tarzan-spirited, there's an aerial tram tour as well.

Current craze

Though St Lucia is no stranger to celebrity visitors, actor Matt Damon recently set tongues wagging when he and wife Luciana Barrosso rented out the entire ultra-luxe Sugar Beach Resort for a vow-renewal ceremony. The star-studded guest list reportedly

included Ben Affleck, Chelsea Clinton, Chris Hemsworth and Gus Van Sant, who partied for three days to the tune of a mid-six-figure price tag.

Trending topics

Who owns the beaches? Can a beach be privatised, or does it belong to everyone? Historically all the beaches are part of the 'Queen's Chain', open to the public even if they're in front of a hotel. But many developers are keen to change this tradition.

The environment has been a hot topic lately, as growing development threatens biodiversity 'hot spots', potentially causing land degradation and species loss.

St Lucia's got all the right stuff for the off-the-beaten-path adventurer

Festival & Events

In May, national and international musicians jam together at the St Lucia Jazz Festival.

In June, St Lucia's Carnival is a bacchanal of street dancers, calypso music, costumes, food and rum.

The Atlantic Rally for Cruisers, a global sailing event, sees enthusiasts arriving in St Lucia in November and December, after sailing 2,700 miles from their embarkation point in Spain.

Random facts

- St Lucia has the highest population-to-Nobel-laureate ratio of any country, with two winners: Arthur Lewis in economics and Derek Walcott in literature.
- Control of the country went back and forth between the British and the French 14 times.
- The national bird, the St Lucia parrot, only exists on the island.
- It is illegal to wear camouflage clothing on St Lucia.

Most bizarre sight

On Pigeon Island, so-called despite the manmade causeway linking it to the rest of St Lucia, visitors will be confronted with photogenically spooky ruins worthy of a Gothic romance novel. Back in the 1550s, the island's first French settler, Jambe de Bois (Wooden Leg), used Pigeon Island as a pirate base. Later, the British turned the island into a fort for use in warfare against the French. Today it's a historic site dripping with vines and thick with the mystery of ages past. ● *By Emily Matchar*

THE UNESCO-LISTED PITON
MOUNTAINS STAND PROUD
ABOVE THE TOWN OF SOUFRIERE

TWO WOMEN STROLL THROUGH THE
COLOURFUL SOUK SEMMARINE

Morocco

Morocco will begin 2015 in high spirits as the country hosts the Africa Cup of Nations, the continent's main soccer championship

ACTIVITIES | ADVENTURE | CULTURE

Population **33 million**
Foreign visitors per year **10 million**
Capital **Rabat**
Languages **Moroccan Arabic (Darija), Berber (main dialects Tashelhit, Tamazight and Tarifit), French**
Major industry **phosphate rock mining and processing**
Unit of currency **dirham (Dh)**
Cost index **glass of beer Dh25 (US$3), two-hour surf lesson Dh300 (US$36); tourist hammam visit and scrub from Dh200 (US$24): tagine in budget restaurant Dh50 (US$6)**

Why go in 2015? > *Soccer and style hit the medina*

Morocco will begin 2015 in high spirits, and not just because the early months of the year draw flocks of tourists to Marrakesh and the south. In January and February, the country hosts the Africa Cup of Nations, the continent's main soccer championship, with matches set to fill stadiums and rattle tagines in Tangier, Rabat, Marrakesh and Agadir. As well as sparking debates over mint tea in cafes from the Mediterranean to the Sahara, the event will be a positive milestone for the relatively stable and progressive North African nation. While the Arab Spring divided many countries in the region, Moroccan pro-democracy

protests sparked reforms and a new constitution, empowering the government but leaving ultimate authority with King Mohammed VI.

Recognising the spell Morocco's winding medina lanes, carpet-piled souks and High Atlas peaks have cast on travellers since the hippy-trail days, the country's tourist industry aimed to attract 10 million visitors annually by 2010. Five years later, the industry is halfway to its next staging post of 2020, hoping to double tourist arrivals to 20 million and become a top-20 destination.

Developments such as budget flights are certainly bringing Morocco's surf beaches, mountain valleys and palm groves closer to Europe. On the ground, travellers can also enjoy increasingly chic accommodation, from medina hideaways to hilltop kasbahs – notably the riad hotels fit for glossy magazines. None of the country's Maghrebi mystique is gone, but travellers can now explore the stirring landscapes and Berber culture in comfort and style. Equally, immersive, community-run tours and homestays offer opportunities to meet Moroccans and learn about their daily lives.

Life-changing experiences

Get lost in the medina. These labyrinthine old quarters, where mopeds and donkeys navigate alleyways and date vendors juggle mobile phones and sales patter, are Morocco's chaotic heart and soul.

Festivals & Events

If you plan to catch the Africa Cup of Nations (17 January to 7 February), bring your own tracksuit and take part in the Marrakesh Marathon, which circuits the city's ramparts in late January.

In June, Fez Festival of World Sacred Music stages performances by *tariqas* (Sufi orders) and World Music stars.

During July's Festival of Popular Arts, the scrum of storytellers, snake-charmers, acrobats and astrologers on Marrakesh's carnivalesque square, Djemaa el-Fna, reaches fever pitch.

One of the year-round religious festivals known as *moussems*, Imilchil Marriage Moussem in September pairs young Berber shepherds with wives.

Hire a turban-wrapped guide and head between the dunes by camel or 4WD to a nomad camp for a night under the stars

Brave the Tizi n'Test pass. Cross one of the notoriously tortuous mountain passes to the snowy peaks of the High Atlas. Mountains such as Jebel Toubkal, North Africa's highest at 4167m, are famous for trekking and climbing, with more opportunities for hiking and village stays in the Middle Atlas, Anti Atlas and Rif ranges.

DAYBREAK NEAR THE
DESERT VILLAGE OF
MERZOUGA

What's Hot...
Historic riads with
hammams, *zellij* tiles
and *tadelakt* walls

What's Not...
Hotels where Hendrix/
Jagger/Burroughs
supposedly stayed
with squat toilets and
crumbling walls

Go in search of white Saharan sands. In Merzouga or M'Hamid, hire a turban-wrapped guide and head between the dunes by camel or 4WD to a nomad camp for a night under the stars. Alternatively, find a shady spot in a date-farming oasis village, or generate more static than a worn carpet when you try sand boarding.

Current craze

Having graced Hollywood movies, Morocco's varied landscapes and atmospheric cities have recently appeared in TV series. In the third season of *Game of Thrones*, Essaouira medina features as Astapor, where Daenerys acquires an army and her dragons fry the city's cruel rulers. Rabat stood in for Tehran in the third season of *Homeland*, and the first season of *Atlantis* was shot around Ouarzazate – already nicknamed 'Ouallywood' for its film studio.

Random facts

■ Casablanca's Hassan II Mosque, one of the world's largest, has a glass floor overlooking the Atlantic waters beneath its rocky perch.
■ Fez medina, a millennium-old maze of souks and tanneries, is the world's largest living Islamic medieval city and most populous car-free urban area.
■ On the Mediterranean coast, Ceuta and Melilla are Spanish-owned enclaves, with plazas, tapas bars and Gaudí-influenced architecture.

Most bizarre sight

Goats climbing frizzy argan trees in the Souss Valley to munch on the nuts.
● *By James Bainbridge*

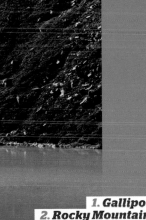

Lonely Planet's Top Ten Regions

THE ICONIC REPLICA
OF THE TROJAN HORSE
IS FOUND NEAR THE
TOWN OF TRUVA

Gallipoli Peninsula, Turkey

The Turks are planning plenty of pomp and circumstance to commemorate the 100th anniversary of the Gallipoli campaign in 1915

CULTURE | ACTIVITIES | EVENTS

Population **Province of Çanakkale 502,000**

Main town **Çanakkale**

Language **Turkish**

Major industries **education, tourism, fishing**

Unit of currency **Turkish lira (₺) but hotels and tours are charged in euros**

Cost index **half-day guided battlefields tour €30 (US$42), full-day private walking tour with guide for small group €250 (US$347), 3-star double hotel room €70 (US$98), 0.33cl Efes beer €3 (US$4.50)**

Why go in 2015?
> *Centenary of the Gallipoli Campaign*

Empires, myths and national identities have been forged in this part of the Aegean for millennia. Close to the ancient city of Troy and on the northwestern side of the strategically important Dardanelles Strait, this slender peninsula (known as Gelibolu in Turkish) has seen more than its fair share of invasions, the most recent being the Allied naval attack on the Dardanelles in March 1915 and the landings of Allied troops at multiple locations on the peninsula on 25 April 1915. Turks see both of these events as important milestones in the development of modern Turkey and are planning plenty of pomp and circumstance to commemorate this year's 100th anniversary, but this episode of history is perhaps even more important to Australians and New Zealanders, who have been visiting Gallipoli in ever-increasing numbers in recent decades. This year they are expected to arrive in their thousands to commemorate the involvement of Anzac (Australian and New Zealand Army Corp) troops in the landing.

It might seem strange that so many people – the vast majority young backpackers – are prepared to cross the world to commemorate an unsuccessful military campaign that occurred long before they were born. But what are being celebrated here are values that the Anzacs are said to have had in spades and that are seen by many Aussies and Kiwis as nation-defining: courage, stamina, laconic humour, mateship and a healthy dose of larrikinism.

British, French and Indian troops also fought valiantly here (over half of the campaign's 57,000 Allied deaths were British, with the landings at Cape Helles being particularly bloody), but until now, few of their countrymen have made the pilgrimage here. This may of course change in

THE ANZAC CEMETERIES IN GALLIPOLI OFFER VISITORS A BEAUTIFUL SETTING FOR THE REMEMBRANCE OF FALLEN SOLDIERS

Festivals & Events

Turks commemorate the Çanakkale naval victory (defeat of the Allied fleet in the Dardanelles) on 18 March. This year, expect naval re-enactments, speeches galore and plenty of partying on Çanakkale's streets.

Around Anzac Day (25 April) there will be Turkish commemorative services at the Turkish 57th Memorial and at Abideis, as well as a French memorial service at Morto Bay and a Commonwealth memorial service at Cape Helles.

So many Australians and New Zealanders were keen to attend the 2015 dawn commemorative service at the Anzac Commemorative Site near Anzac Cove on 25 April that the two governments were forced to run official ballots for tickets. 10,000 seats have now been allocated, and every hotel room in the region is already booked.

Those Australians who were unsuccessful in the ballot may get a second opportunity to attend an official commemorative service on 6 August at Lone Pine, site of some of the campaign's most fierce fighting.

this centenary year, as senior British politicians and members of the royal family will be attending commemoration ceremonies, and events are likely to receive considerable media attention.

Life-changing experiences

History buffs will be in their element here. The Troy Archaeological Park and its brand-new museum (opening mid-2015) hold court on one side of the Dardanelles, and memorials and a whizz-bang interactive museum interpret the battlefields on the other. Both can be visited on half-day guided tours offered by a clutch of local companies, but the battlefields deserve more time (think about taking a day-long walking tour as well). A short ferry ride away is the Aegean island of Gökçeada, aka ancient Imbros, where hauntingly beautiful abandoned Greek villages await exploration and expansive beaches attract windsurfers from across Europe – we suggest staying here or in Çanakkale rather than in the ugly town of Eceabat.

Trending topic

Growing interest from Turks, Australians and New Zealanders means that visitor numbers to the battlefields are skyrocketing, and there is growing concern about the adverse impact that crowds are having on the landscape, which is officially protected as the Gallipoli Peninsula Historical National Park. The Turkish memorials in particular can be horrendously crowded on weekends between March and September, and we are sorry to report that tacky souvenir and fast-food stands are imparting an inappropriately carnival atmosphere. Even more concerning has been the widening of roads to accommodate fleets of tour buses, compromising the physical integrity of important sites including Anzac Cove.

● *By Virginia Maxwell*

MARVEL AT THE STILLNESS OF
DREAM LAKE IN THE ROCKY
MOUNTAIN NATIONAL PARK

Rocky Mountain National Park, USA

In 2015, Rocky Mountain National Park celebrates its 100th anniversary. Come along and join in the patriotic fun

ACTIVITIES | ADVENTURE | OFF-ROAD

Population **1000 (elk, that is)**
Visitors per year **3.1 million**
Main town **Estes Park**
Language **English**
Major industry **tourism**
Unit of currency **US dollar (US$)**
Cost index **entrance fee US$20 per car, US$10 per pedestrian, campsite at Moraine Park Campground US$20, 'Hiking Rocky Mountain National Park' guidebook US$17, post-hike burger and beer in Estes Park US$10**

Why go in 2015?
> *Centenary blowout means partying like its 1915*

These snowy peaks, wildflower-carpeted meadows and mirror-like mountain lakes define the glory of the American West. Here you'll find herds of grazing elk, icy rivers teeming with silvery trout, high-altitude forests of fragrant Douglas fir trees, snowy tundra camouflaging white-tailed ptarmigan. This is a hiker's heaven, with 355 miles of trails, including several winding their way towards the summit of Longs Peak, the park's famed '14er' (mountain higher than 14,000ft). In winter, you can experience almost any snow-related activity in existence – sledding, skiing, snowshoeing.

In 2015, Rocky Mountain celebrates its 100th anniversary. Expect special speakers, activities and community events, art exhibitions, concerts of mountain-themed songs and a parade of vintage Ford Model Ts along the park's highway. So come along and join in the patriotic fun in one of America's most rugged and thrilling national parks.

Life-changing experiences

Drive Trail Ridge Road, America's highest continuous paved road. Described as a 'highway to the sky', it travels above the tree line to 12,183ft. Goggle at the jagged, glacier-covered mountaintops, all from the safety of your car.

Spot a moose meandering through the willow thickets of the Kawuneeche Valley, on the park's west side.

Hike Mt Ida, one of the lesser-known yet most stunning trails in the Rockies. Expect pristine mountain tundra, with a view of Longs Peak in the distance. In summer, wildflowers turn the high meadows into a rainbow carpet.

Trending topics

Recent studies have suggested that pollution is altering the ecosystem of Rocky Mountain National Park in subtle but potentially permanent ways. Emissions from cars, planes, factories and farms rise up into the mountains, decreasing plant abundance in ways only obvious

Festivals & Events

26 January marks the 100th anniversary of President Woodrow Wilson's signing the bill that created Rocky Mountain National Park. The park will celebrate with – what else? – a giant community birthday party.

From 10 to 16 August, Plein Air Rockies exhibits the best in Western landscape painting, in the visitors centre in Estes Park. Expect workshops, music, food and prizes.

In August, runners in the Rocky Mountain Half Marathon test their lung capacity on the high-elevation route along the border of the park. Join them for some major quad-burn.

Snowy peaks, wildflower-carpeted meadows and mirror-like mountain lakes define the glory of the American West

A STONE CHURCH STANDS AMID THE NATURAL BEAUTY OF COLORADO'S ROCKY MOUNTAINS

the park. Today's herd of some 30 to 50 is descended from moose relocated from Wyoming in 1978.

Most bizarre sight

The abandoned mining settlement of Lulu City is a classic Western ghost town. Built during the silver rush of the late 1870s and 1880s, it's now a handful of decayed cabins and crumbled foundations amid the wild pines of the Kawuneeche Valley. What's that you hear? It could be the wind. Or maybe it's the thwack of a long-dead miner's pickaxe?

Local lingo

Hardcore mountain

to scientists – for now. If unchecked, they could acidify soil and damage lakes and rivers as well. As the population of Colorado grows, the problem is likely to become more serious. So visit now, and support local environmental efforts.

Random facts

■ The Stanley Hotel in Estes Park was Stephen King's inspiration for *The Shining*. The hotel shows the famously terrifying movie version on a continuous loop on Channel 42 in all guest rooms.
■ The Grand Lake Cemetery, in use since 1892, is one of the few active graveyards within a US national park.
■ By the 1970s, there were almost no moose within

people – climbers, hikers, ski bums – have their own lingo, which may seem like Greek to flatlanders (that's the rest of us). 'Peakbagging', for example, is the activity of trying to complete a certain set of mountain summits – the 10 highest peaks in Rocky Mountain National Park, say, or all the 14ers in Colorado (there are 53). If you plan on peakbagging, know that a 'technical climb' means you need special gear like ropes or crampons to make the summit – Longs Peak is technical most of the year. And remember, the 'vertical rise' of a hike is the amount of elevation gain between the trailhead and the summit – ie, how much your thighs will ache the next day. ● *By Emily Matchar*

WONDER AT THE NATURAL
SPECTACLE OF TOLEDO'S
TIGER CAVE IN RIO BLANCO
NATIONAL PARK

The Toledo District, Belize

Trek out to the partially excavated tombs and pyramids of Nim Li Punnit and Lubaantun and on most days it'll just be you, the jungle and the ghosts of the past for miles around

OFF-ROAD | CULTURE | ADVENTURE

Population **30,500**

Visitors per year **25,000**

Main town **Punta Gorda**

Languages **English, Maya, Garifuna**

Major industries **agriculture, some tourism**

Unit of currency **BZ dollar (BZ$)**

Cost index **meal on the street BZ$6 (US$3), meal at resort BZ$30–40 (US$15–20), shared bunkroom at Rio Blanco Ranger Station BZ$20 (US$10), cottage at eco-resort BZ$200–1000 (US$100–500)**

Why go in 2015?

> **Walk the road less travelled before the road comes here**

With gorgeous islands, protected jungles and ancient Maya ruins, it's no wonder that the small Central American nation of Belize welcomes 300,000 visitors annually. But though Belize's Toledo District possesses all these splendours and more, only a single-digit percent of visitors to Belize ever make it to the deep south. Thank geography for that: Toledo sits at the end of the Southern Highway, making it Belize's only dead-end district, still largely the province of adventure travellers willing to go the distance to experience the country as it was in days gone by.

But as Bob Dylan once sang, *the times they are a-changin'*, and Toledo's days as a backwater are almost certainly coming to a close as the $8 million asphalt road – which, when completed, will form part of the Pan-American Highway – continues to be built from the Southern Highway towards the border of Guatemala. Once the road reaches the tiny village of Jalacte, Belize's third (and Toledo's only) international border crossing will open, connecting Toledo's tiny Maya villages with neighbouring Guatemala and the world beyond.

What changes the road will bring to the area is uncertain, but 2015 is likely to be among the last years in which Toledo remains off the beaten path.

As of mid-2014, the road was paved just until Rio Blanco National Park, a protected wildlife area with waterfalls, hiking trails, and Belize's most beautiful swimming hole. From the park, it's less than 15 miles through jungle and Maya villages over a rough and unpaved (for now) dirt road to Jalacte, site of the future border crossing.

> **Most people are worried that their traditional way of life may be eroded by the creation of this highway**

TRADITIONAL VILLAGE HOUSES
OF BELIZE'S TOLEDO DISTRICT
EVOKE BYGONE TIMES

Life-changing experiences

Take a jungle hike through the stunning Rio Blanco National Park followed by a swim in the protected wildlife area's crystal blue waterfall-fed pond.

Learn the ancient and delicious Maya tradition of cacao production and chocolate-making at Ixcacao Maya Belizean Chocolate (formerly known as Cyrila's), sampling along the way chocolate bars, hot chocolate, cacao wine and more.

Snorkel and scuba dive in the Sapodilla Marine Reserve or the Snake Cayes, a chain of tiny, protected islands in southern Belize undiscovered by tourists.

Festivals & Events

Celebrated in the village of Blue Creek, Toledo's Maya Day celebration will be held on Sunday 22 March 2015.

Like chocolate? Then you won't want to miss the Chocolate Festival of Belize (formerly the Toledo Cacao Festival), which will happen on Commonwealth Day weekend (22 to 24 May 2015) in Punta Gorda.

Bringing together drummers from around the country, Punta Gorda's Battle of the Drums weekend will happen from 13 to 15 November 2015.

Study traditional Creole and Garifuna music and drum-making with Emmeth Young or Ronald Raymond McDonald, two master drummers who have schools in Punta Gorda.

Defining difference

Those who make it to Toledo will catch a glimpse of Belize as it existed in decades gone by. While most of the Maya villages in the deep south have electricity (many through solar power), meals and accommodation in San Pedro Columbia, San Antonio and San Jose will likely be with local Maya families rather than guesthouses. Trek out to the partially excavated tombs and pyramids of Nim Li Punnit and Lubaantun and on most days it'll just be you, the jungle and the ghosts of the past for miles around. You may run into fellow travellers in Punta Gorda (Toledo's largest – and only – town), but even there you'll experience none of the tourist-town vibe of Caye Caulker or Cayo.

Trending topics

That the building of the Pan-American Highway will bring major change to the region is a given. Christopher Nesbitt, founder of Toledo-based Maya Mountain Research Farm (which promotes economic security and environmental conservation throughout Belize), has spent much time in recent months working with villagers along the new road to develop solar and other sustainable forms of power to cope with the coming increase in traffic and visitors. 'People in the Maya communities are all talking about the changes the road will bring,' says Christopher. 'Increased traffic will bring some benefits, but most people are worried that their traditional way of life may be eroded by the creation of this highway.'

● *By Joshua Samuel Brown*

SAVOUR THE TRANQUILLITY
OF THE TARKINE
WILDERNESS IN TASMANIA

Tasmania, Australia

In 2015, Tasmania will open the second stage of Australia's premier coastal bushwalking experience, the Three Capes Track. This stage will take in some of the stunning sea cliffs of the Tasman National Park

| ADVENTURE | EVENTS | FOOD |

Population **513,000**

Foreign visitors per year **1 million**

Main town **Hobart**

Language **English**

Major industries **forestry, mining, agriculture, tourism**

Unit of currency **Australian dollar (A$)**

Cost index **entry to MONA A$20 (US$18.75), cheese plate at Jam Packed Cafe at Henry Jones Art Hotel A$16 (US$15), Bronze Pass for Port Arthur Historic Site A$35 (US$32.80), Attic Room at the Islington Hotel, Hobart A$395 (US$370)**

4

→ **Why go in 2015?** › *Ripe for the picking*

Wild and dramatic, cultured and quirky, isolated yet accessible – Australia's island state, nestled comfortably at the southeastern base of Australia, is intrinsic to the nation's story. Van Diemen's Land (as Tasmania was christened by white settlers) was home to some of the first convict ships to land in Australia, and the tragic, harrowing and haunting tales of those arrivals permeate the state. The Port Arthur Historic Site, a former penal colony, serves as a beautiful and disquieting reminder of the region's brutal past.

However, modern Tasmania has emancipated itself from wallowing in the

past and adopted a fresh, hip and inclusive attitude sparked by the brilliant revival of its now super-cool waterfront capital, Hobart, and the development of an eclectic year-long events calendar.

Offering some of Australia's most diverse, remote and wild outdoor experiences, Tasmania abounds in natural splendour. Whether it's exploring the quiet, eerie grandeur of Cradle Mountain, bravely traversing the mighty Franklin River – home to the state's dark forested heart, or stumbling upon the breathtaking beaches that make up the Bay of Fires, the state contains a lifetime's worth of adventures.

In 2015, Tasmania will open the second stage of Australia's premier coastal bushwalking experience, the Three Capes Track. This stage will link Denman's Cove, opposite Port Arthur, with Cape Huay, via 35km of redeveloped walking track which take in some of the stunning sea cliffs of the Tasman National Park, where white-breasted sea eagles soar above the ocean. One of the largest projects of its kind to be undertaken anywhere in the world, once the third stage is completed the track will offer walkers a multiday bushwalking and boating experience which can be taken independently or with a guided tour operator.

Life-changing experiences

The diversity of offerings from Tasmania's plate may require multiple helpings. Descend the spiralled

Festivals & Events

Mona foma (festival of music and art) kicks off Tasmania's event calendar in style every January, when an Eminent Artist in Residence joins former Violent Femmes bassist, Brian Ritchie, in delivering Australia's most eclectic cultural festival.

'Inspire, entertain, enliven' is the motto for a reinvention of the biennial international arts festival known as Ten Days on the Island, which will take place in late March 2015.

Brightening the darker winter months from April to August, the Lumina Festival umbrellas over 100 cultural, food and wine events.

Hungry? Hit Hobart's waterfront across New Year's Eve week for the Taste Festival and sample the Apple Isle's best seafood, wine and cheese.

From around 29 December the sleek vessels competing in the annual Sydney to Hobart Yacht Race start arriving into Hobart's Salamanca Wharf.

Offering some of Australia's most diverse, remote and wild outdoor experiences, Tasmania abounds in natural splendour

HIKE UP A ROCKY GRANITE TRACK FOR A VIEW OF WINEGLASS BAY YOU WON'T FORGET

staircase of Hobart's uber-trendy subterranean MONA (Museum of Old and New Art) located in the belly of the Moorilla Winery to discover the treasures within. Explore one of the world's most significant temperate rainforests on a multiday trek through the Tarkine Wilderness. Watch sea birds take flight as you sea-kayak at dusk in Coles Bay (bordering popular Freycinet National Park).

Trending topic

You can't escape it – the debate over logging and the economy it supports versus the conservation and preservation of the pristine Tasmanian wilderness is a hot topic on the island. Everyone you talk to will have a strong and passionate opinion on the subject.

Most bizarre sight

The gothic grandeur of Australia's oldest continually functioning brewery, the Cascade Brewery in South Hobart, never fails to draw a gasp on first sight. Ominously stretching towards the sky, it's a structure that suggests the setting of a terrifying horror film rather than the reality, the Willy Wonka-esque home of one of Australia's favourite adult brews.

Regional flavours

The Tassie food scene is a gourmet's paradise, best

exemplified by the diversity of produce found in the wilds of Bruny Island. The isolation and stunning coastal scenery of this island in the state's southeast make it the perfect escape from the rat race, but it's the artisanal produce that can be sourced here that elevates it to must-go. Whether it's getting a frisky fill of oysters at Get Shucked Oyster Farm, downing a few glasses of pinot noir at Australia's most southern winery, or gorging on freshly picked berries from the local berry farm, there's no better place to taste Tassie on a plate.

● *By Chris Zeiher*

A REINDEER ANTLER
LIES NEAR ALKEHORNET
IN ARCTIC NORWAY

Northern Norway

Land of the midnight sun and the wizard's wand spectacle of the aurora borealis, Northern Norway is where the wild things are – in more ways than one

ADVENTURE | CULTURE | FOOD

Population **462,908**
Foreign visitors per year **520,000**
Main town **Tromsø**
Languages **Norwegian, Sami**
Major industries **oil and gas, aquaculture, minerals, tourism**
Unit of currency **Norwegian krone (Nkr)**
Cost index **glass of Arctic Beer Nkr60 (US$10), hotel double per night Nkr750–1400 (US$125–233), Sami reindeer hide Nkr500 (US$83), dog-sledding excursion Nkr1250 (US$208)**

Why go in 2015? > A total eclipse in Svalbard

Hey, who turned out the lights? Land of the midnight sun and the wizard's wand spectacle of the aurora borealis, Northern Norway is always light fantastic, but in 2015 all light will disappear totally for a couple of minutes when the moon blocks out the sun. Put 20 March in your diary and book your ticket to this epic blackout. The best place to witness one of the most stunning celestial events of the century? The frozen wilderness of Svalbard, an archipelago midway between Norway and the North Pole, where polar bears outnumber people. Miss the total solar eclipse and you've got a long wait – the next one in Europe will be in 2026.

Speaking of light, the high activity of the aurora borealis is set to continue in 2015, with solar winds interacting with charged particles in the earth's magnetic field frequently illuminating the polar sky. Luck, cloudless skies and the new NorwayLights app are what you need to glimpse this natural phenomenon. The flickers of purple, swirls of gold and flashes of green are like the strobe lights of Norse gods at a heavenly rave.

Not only the weather is cool north of the Arctic Circle in Norway. Base yourself in party-loving Tromsø, home to the world's northernmost university, to hit some of its happening jazz bars after a day spent reindeer sledding. Bodø, too, is both gorgeously remote and surprisingly hip, with new-wave Scandi restaurants like Smak reinventing the culinary scene, clubs like Dama Di ramping up the nightlife and London-based street artist Phlegm making a splash on the city streets. Northern Norway is where the wild things are in more ways than one.

Life-changing experiences

Northern Norway is going to blow your mind with its heartbreakingly beautiful landscapes of glaciers and fjord-riven mountains, all bathed in crystal-clear light. Welcome to one of Europe's last great wildernesses. Experiences like crossing the Arctic Circle as the aurora borealis comes out to play, spotting polar bears – not too close, mind – on the icy tundra

Northern Norway is going to blow your mind with its heartbreakingly beautiful landscapes of glaciers and fjord-riven mountains

of Spitsbergen and eating reindeer stew in a fire-warmed Sami *lavoo* tent will be etched on your memory for ever more. Spend a while lapping up the gentle island pace in Kjerringøy, watching sea eagles wheel and whales splash around in the ocean in the Tolkienesque Lofoten Islands, and hiking in the glacial grandeur of the Saltfjellet-Svartisen National Park and you may never want to leave, we swear.

Most bizarre sight

As natural phenomena go, Saltstraumen plays in the premier league. Like the whirlpool of Nordic giants, this soul-stirring wonder is the world's strongest tidal current, with 400 million cu metres of water rushing through a sound that links two fjords at speeds of up to 20 knots (37km/h). For a thrill, notch up the speed bouncing past it at close range in a RIB (rigid inflatable boat), with the silver-grey ripple of mountains a beautiful blur on the horizon.

Defining difference

Where the northern lights shine so too does Sami culture. The indigenous Sami have been in Northern Norway longer than anyone, their lives shaped by the seasons and the migratory patterns of reindeer herding. Technological advances

Festivals & Events

The Sami host a week of traditional festivities in early February – the highlight is the reindeer-racing championships.

Spandex-clad runners hit the streets of Tromsø at 70°N for the Midnight Sun Marathon in late June.

Bodø swings into summer at the Nordland Music Festival in August, a 10-day bash of classical, jazz, rock and folk music.

You'll need to slip into a dry-suit and dive into the frozen sea to catch king crab in Kirkenes from December to April, but it might just be the best crab you've ever tasted.

COLOURED WOODEN HOUSES NEAR LONGYEARBYEN IN SVALBARD

(snowmobiles and helicopters to track reindeer, for instance) aside, the Sami way of life remains rooted in tradition. They have their own language, parliament, dress and dwellings – the tepee-like, reindeer-skin-clad *lavoo*. If you're lucky enough to be invited into one, you'll probably be treated to a *joik* or two. Sung from the heart, these soulful, enigmatic poems are often odes to friends and family, defined more by rhythm than rhyme.

Regional flavours

Reindeer, stewed Sami-style with juniper berries, wild mushrooms, sour cream and thyme (*finnbiff*), or roast (*reinsdyrstek*), is a red-meat treat, as are elk burgers and steaks. An oddity on the Norwegian breakfast table, *brunost* is a cheese that is, well, not *actually* cheese but sweetish, brownish, fudgy whey. Yum, huh? Simply slice and layer onto dense rye bread. The fish from icy Arctic waters are top quality, and just-caught cod and salmon never taste better than simply grilled on an open fire and served by a fjord. Cloudberries (*moltebær*) are the one thing that is worth braving mosquito-infested swamps for, locals say. These golden berries make wickedly tangy mousses and ice creams. Polish off a meal with aquavit, a caraway-flavoured potato liqueur.

● *By Kerry Christiani*

ENJOY THE BREATHTAKING VIEW OF HIMALAYAN MOUNTAINS, LAKES AND GLACIERS FROM GOKYO RI

Khumbu, Nepal

With 2015 marking a half-century since Major Jimmy Roberts organised the first commercial trek in Nepal, it might just be time to dust off those trekking boots

ACTIVITIES   ADVENTURE   CULTURE

Population **106,000 (Solu-Khumbu district)**
Foreign trekkers per year **35,000**
Main town **Namche Bazaar**
Languages **Sherpa (similar to Tibetan), Nepali**
Major industries **tourism, mountaineering, agriculture (yaks and potatoes)**
Unit of currency **Nepali rupee (Rs)**
Cost index **set meal of *dal bhat* (rice and vegetables) Rs 400 (US$4), lodge room for a night Rs 300–700 (US$3–7), porter-guide Rs 2000 (US$20) per day, permit to climb Mt Everest US$10,000**

Why go in 2015? > The trek of a lifetime

We don't really need to sell you on the mountain glories of the Khumbu region; just a whisper of the word 'Everest' and everyone in the room snaps to attention. The chances are that if you love the mountains, you've always considered walking to Everest. It's the ultimate goal of the vertically inclined, a classic journey in the footsteps of Tenzing and Hillary into the planet's most jaw-dropping mountain arena, home to the world's highest peak but encompassing so much more.

Now that Nepal's Maoist uprising is firmly behind it, trekkers are once again rediscovering the region's remoter trails. For an alternative to the standard

Festivals & Events

Mani Rimdu is the most famous Sherpa festival, celebrating the victory of Buddhism over the local Bon religion with three days of colourful masked dances. The big celebration is at Tengboche Monastery (November), with a quieter alternative at Thame Monastery (May).

Tibetan opera, masked dances and home-brewed *chang* (barley beer) add a buzz to the Sherpa New Year festivities in February.

The magician and Tantric master Guru Rinpoche (Padmasambhava) is revered as a second Buddha throughout much of the Himalaya and his birthday is celebrated with religious processions and prayer ceremonies during summer's Dumje festival (June or July).

Base Camp route try the high-altitude Three Passes trek or adventurous Mera Peak expedition. If you want something more authentic, tread the old-school approach routes to Everest from Jiri and Tumlingtar, along parts of the 1700km-long Great Himalaya Trail.

Already popular, the trails to Everest are only going to get busier in future seasons. With 2015 marking a half-century since Major Jimmy Roberts organised the first commercial trek in Nepal, it might just be time to dust off those trekking boots. Why trek to Everest? Well, as Mallory famously quipped, 'because it's there'. And because life is now.

Life-changing experiences

Pack your head torch for the sunrise views of Mt Everest and the Khumbu Icefall from 5545m Kala Pattar.

Beat the Base Camp crowds and acclimatise slowly by taking a side trail to the stunning scenery of the Gokyo and Chukkhung valleys, or to the Sherpa villages of Thame and Khunde.

Attend one of the daily talks on altitude sickness at the Himalayan Rescue Association in Pheriche – it might just save your life.

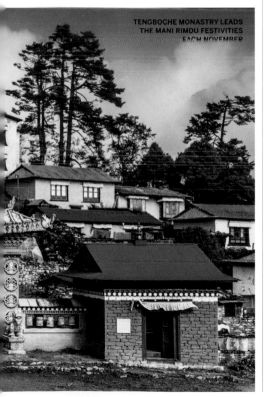

TENGBOCHE MONASTRY LEADS THE MANI RIMDU FESTIVITIES EACH NOVEMBER

Trending topics

Sherpa safety and working conditions, after 16 Sherpas died together on the Khumbu Icefall in 2014.

With 60 flights a day arriving at Lukla airport in peak season and 200 people queuing up to attempt Everest on a good day, overcrowding on the trails is an ever-pressing issue. Finding a sustainable way to deal with the waste produced by so many trekkers and porters in such a remote region is a complex problem, though solar-powered technology is making a difference in many trekking lodges. Since 2014 each Everest climber is now required to carry 8kg of waste off the mountain.

Air safety is another concern, after air crashes in 2010, 2011 and 2012 killed dozens of trekkers and Nepali staff en route to or from the region.

Random facts

- At Everest Base Camp you are breathing in only 50% of the oxygen available at sea level.
- Over 3000 people have summitted Mt Everest since Tenzing and Hillary reached the top in 1953: the youngest aged 13, the oldest 81.

Most bizarre sight

Fans of the bizarre will want to hike up to Khumjung Monastery to get a peek at its yeti scalp. Nearby Pangboche Monastery had its famous yeti hand stolen in 1991, but a replica is now on display.

Defining difference

The local Sherpa people are what make trekking in the Everest region such a joy. Many of the lodges you stay in will be run by a retired summitteer and most families have at least one member employed as a climbing porter or trekking guide. Sherpa culture also gives the region its distinctly Tibetan flavour, adorning the grand landscapes with stupas, prayer flags and stones carved with Buddhist mantras. ● *By Bradley Mayhew*

THE ICONIC FERROCARRIL
CHIHUAHUA PACÍFICO RAILWAY
TRAVERSES COPPER CANYON

Copper Canyon, Mexico

Rearing up out of the North Mexico desert in a blaze of green only to drop away again into canyons many times greater than Arizona's Grand Canyon, this place is arrestingly beautiful

ACTIVITIES | ADVENTURE | OFF-ROAD

Population **175,000**
Foreign visitors per year **200,000**
Main town **Creel**
Languages **Spanish, Rarámuri**
Major industries **tourism, agriculture**
Unit of currency **Mexican peso (M$)**
Cost index **hotel double/dorm M$700/150 (US$55/11), day's mountain-bike hire M$300 (US$23), four-person canyon tour M$2300 (US$175), second-class Chihuahua–Copper Canyon–Los Mochis train ride M$1442 (US$109)**
Topography **deepest canyon depth (1849m), highest point (3306m)**

Why go in 2015? > Accessible adventures

Run for your life, bike for your life, or – for real daredevils – be blasted out over a 1250m-deep precipice: the Copper Canyon was never short on thrills but its list is lengthening in 2015.

The big reason for the changes is the new Creel Airport, finally set to get off the ground running connections to Houston and Dallas in the US, as well as prominent Mexican destinations like Mexico City and Cancún. Traditionally, visiting the canyons has been an undertaking of several days – approaching via the classic but time-consuming Ferrocarril Chihuahua Pacífico rail route and letting off steam with an into-the-wild odyssey of canyon rim-to-bottom hiking. Now travellers can get the 'wow' without the 'ow'.

Creative tour companies will have opened by 2015 a Tarahumara running trip (far-off-road running with the region's most distinctive indigenous people, the Tarahumara), and biking down the hair-raising but newly paved road to Batopilas, a colonial town hidden in the tropical canyon valleys. The canyons' rim-straddling adventure park, Parque de Aventura Barrancas del Cobre, is adding a brace of new adrenaline highs too: the world's longest zip line, and a slingshot ride – which casts you out into the middle of the canyon on a bungee before reeling you squealing back in. Come in, get your canyon fix and get out: far more quickly than ever before.

What's Hot...
Tarahumara immersion experiences, paved roads (well, a little bit), anyone who finishes the Copper Canyon's ultra-marathon

What's Not...
Express trains, marijuana plantation bust-ups

Life-changing experiences
Ride the rails on Mexico's best train journey from the desert (Chihuahua) through the canyons to the Pacific coast (Los Mochis).

Steel yourself for a cross-canyon whoosh on the world's longest zip line at Parque de Aventura Barrancas del Cobre.

See the canyons from the clouds with the brand new helicopter tours offered by Creel-based outfit the 3Amigos.

Current craze
Flashpackers are replacing the backpackers of old among the canyons' tourist clientele and that trend is likely to continue,

as sampling the cream of the outdoor offerings here is nowhere near as cheap as it was. Add a session at the adventure park onto the price of a train ride, factor in that soon there will be more zip lines and snazzier hotels (planned for the canyon bottom) and you'll see why it's well-heeled thrill-seekers checking in.

Defining difference
The remote peaks and troughs of the Copper Canyon are a refuge not only for the Tarahumara (best-known for their legendary long-distance running abilities over hundreds of kilometres and 1500m+ elevation gains) but also many of Mexico's Mennonites (a fair-haired, often blue-eyed people tracing their roots to 16th-century Holland, best-known for their farming prowess which yields, among other things, delicious cheeses). Such cultures lend more colour to a region that, rearing

TRAIL-RUNNING AT
TARAHUMARA – A FEARSOME
TEST OF FITNESS AND STAMINA

Festivals & Events

March sees the epic Ultra Marathon Caballo Blanco, a 50-mile lung-buster of a race across unadulterated wilderness and your chance to compete with Tarahumara runners. Get training…

Running from March to July in locations across Chihuahua state is the Festival Internacional de Turismo Aventura (International Adventure Tourism Festival). Expect extreme dune events in the desert – or catch a trout festival in Madera just north of the canyons.

Festival Internacional Chihuahua takes place in the city of the same name throughout September, focusing on the region's musical heritage.

up out of the North Mexico desert in a blaze of green only to drop away again into canyons many times greater than Arizona's Grand Canyon, would already be arrestingly beautiful.

Most bizarre sight

Cuauhtémoc, a stop that the already eccentric-looking old steam train El Chepe makes on the Ferrocarril Chihuahua Pacífico just before Creel, is a pretty singular city. It's home to the vast majority of Mexico's Mennonites who arrived here from Canada in the 1920s, and wear clothes reminiscent of an earlier century. The men are usually seen in loose-fitting overalls and the women attire themselves in long dark dresses and headscarves. They speak a dialect of Low German, and still do most agricultural work with equipment worthy of being acquisitioned by a museum in most countries. ● *By Luke Waterson*

By 2015, creative tour companies will have opened far-off-road running trips with the region's most distinctive indigenous people, the Tarahumara

THE MIGHTY KOMODO
DRAGON, INDONESIA'S
MOST ICONIC INHABITANT

Flores, Indonesia

With newly improved airports and better roads, Flores offers great overland adventure but doesn't require any survival skills to do so

ACTIVITIES | ADVENTURE | OFF-ROAD

Population **1.9 million**
Main town **Labuanbajo**
Language **Indonesian**
Major industries **tourism, agriculture, fishing**
Unit of currency **rupiah (Rp)**
Cost index **double room in guesthouse 400,000Rp (US$40), Bintang beer 20,000Rp (US$2), daytrip from Labuanbajo to Komodo National Park 250,000Rp (US$25), car and driver per day 6,000,000Rp (US$60)**

Why go in 2015? > Indonesia's next great journey

Start with the dragons and end with picture-perfect beaches, in between enjoy great diving, lush tropical forests, smoking volcanoes, stunning hikes, exotic cultures and some of Asia's best pizza (really!). Indonesia's Flores packs a lot into an island only 380km long west to east. Now with newly improved airports (there are numerous flights a day from Bali) and better roads (though they do still curve like mad), Flores offers great overland adventure but doesn't require any survival skills to do so.

In the west, Labuanbajo is a laid-back port town made for travellers: cafes, guesthouses, bars, dive shops and some great restaurants (get that incredible

A VIVID TURQUOISE LAKE
IN FLORES' KELIMUTU
NATIONAL PARK

pizza at Made in Italy), all with just enough funkiness to preclude feeling packaged. To the west Komodo National Park is home to the huge namesake man-eating lizards (aka dragons). Rinca, a park island close to Labuanbajo, has just had a major revamp that includes new visitor facilities.

Heading east across Flores, there are new tourist offices, cafes and guesthouses in the towns and small cities such as Bajawa and Moni that you pass through on the trans-Flores highway. Road improvements mean you can easily divert to see a newly erupting volcano, an isolated beach or one of the hidden villages of the island's diverse and ancient cultures.

Life-changing experiences

In only a week you can revel in an overload of experiences. Start in Labuanbajo, gazing worriedly at the other-worldly dragons, then stop off at one of the perfect beaches on any of many nearby tiny islands. Toss in some of Indonesia's best diving and snorkelling. Get a public mini-bus or private car and head west up and over, in and around the island's ever-varied landscape. Stop off in places like the cute mountain town of Bajawa, where you can visit the Ngada people's village of Bena.

Onwards east, the steamy port city of Ende is

bracketed by perfectly conical and often smouldering volcanoes. Pause at the traveller-friendly hamlet of Moni for a day to see the sunrise over triple lakes at Kelimutu – each a different vivid colour, from turquoise to orange. The next day, stop at Paga's pristine beach before finishing in Maumere. This trip is literally a kaleidoscope of experiences you'll still be digesting months later.

> **This trip is literally a kaleidoscope of experiences you'll still be digesting months later**

Festivals & Events

Like a vision from the past, the village of Bena reflects the ancient culture of the Ngada. Rows of dramatically thatched houses face megalithic tombs. Always welcoming and always worth a visit, you'll be especially rewarded if you make the six-day Reba ceremony in late December or January featuring dancing, feasting, sacrifices and ebony black costumes.

Random facts

The Komodo dragon (*ora*) is a monitor lizard, albeit one on steroids. Growing up to 3m in length, random encounters are a bad idea. Some dragon details:

■ They are omnivorous, and enjoy eating their young.

■ Bacteria in the dragon's mouth is its secret weapon. One bite from a dragon leads to septic infections that inevitably kill the victim. The huge lizard lopes along after its victim waiting for it to die, which can take up to two weeks.

■ There is no accepted reason that the dragons are only found around Flores although it's thought that their ancestors came from Australia 4 million years ago.

Most bizarre sight

Flores offers a lot of tough competition for this label, but you'll likely stare in mute wonder at the vast rice fields laid out in the shape of spiderwebs near Cancar.

Regional flavours

An ever-growing number of cafes aimed at visitors offer up all manner of fresh, creative and often organic meals. Freshly caught seafood figures on many menus while in towns and cities Indonesian classics and the ever-changing *nasi campur* (dish of the day) are cheap and tasty.

● *By Ryan Ver Berkmoes*

↑

What's Hot...
Labuanbajo is right on the cusp: an inviting town that's an ideal base for Flores adventures but which hasn't yet sold its soul – and mellow vibe – to tourism

———

...What's Not
Maumere is a bookend to a Flores trip: fly into Labuanbajo, fly out of Maumere. But it's a dud to visit, so you'll just want a quick night there before your early morning flight back to Bali

↓

**THE ONLY WAY IS DOWN:
SANDBOARDING IN THE
MAGNIFICENT ATACAMA DESERT**

Atacama Desert, Chile

With so many natural attractions within easy reach of the village of San Pedro de Atacama, the only problem is that you won't have enough time to see and do everything in this dreamlike desert

ACTIVITIES | ADVENTURE | OFF-ROAD

Population **292,054**
Main town **Copiapó**
Language **Spanish**
Major industry **mining**
Unit of currency **Chilean peso (Ch$)**
Cost index **pisco sour Ch$1500–2500 (US$3–5), hotel double Ch$44,000–105,000 (US$80–180), day trip to El Tatio geysers Ch$20,000–30,000 (US$36–54)**

9

Why go in 2015? > *Stars in your eyes*

'What makes the desert beautiful,' says the little prince in Antoine de Saint-Exupéry's famed 1943 novella, 'is that somewhere it hides a well.' Indeed, it was a deep recess in the earth that brought the world's attention to the Atacama in 2010, when a collapsed mine trapped 33 Chilean miners underground for more than two months. After their miraculous rescue, Hollywood jumped on the story, trooping camera crews and movie stars through the desert in 2014 to film the adventure flick *The 33*.

The subterranean drama set the stage for exciting developments in the opposite space – the stunningly clear skies high above the sun-parched desert.

Festivals & Events

In early January, celebrate the first full moon of the year at Kunza Raymi ('Our party' in a phrase combining Quechua and Kunza, the native language of the desert's original ethnic group). New on the region's cultural calendar, the mystical outdoor festival features live music, club-style parties, and camping under the stars.

The last days of June bring one of the year's biggest public celebrations, the Fiesta de San Pedro y San Pablo (Feast of St Peter and St Paul). Honouring the patron saint of the village of San Pedro, the weeklong religious festival culminates on 29 June, when colourful ceremonial dancers take over the streets as the sun rises.

In the Atacama, locals make their annual offerings to Pachamama ('earth mother' to indigenous groups throughout the Andes) on 1 August – the *'pago'* (payment) to the goddess involves tributes of special foods, drinks, and coca leaves.

In cooperation with major research foundations in Europe, East Asia and the United States, Chile has launched ALMA (the Atacama Large Millimeter/submillimeter Array), the largest astronomical project in existence. The high-precision radio antennae of this revolutionary observatory, perched atop a 5000m plateau, are drawing astronomers and scientists from around the world to study the formation of stars and planets.

With fascinating astronomer-led stargazing tours leaving nightly from the village of San Pedro de Atacama – ground zero for outdoor adventure in this psychedelic desert landscape – there's never been a better time to make the voyage to the driest desert in the world. Peering up into the night sky, the immense view might conjure another line from

The Little Prince. 'All the stars are a bloom with flowers...'

Life-changing experiences

From adrenaline-fueled adventures – ascending a high-altitude volcano, sandboarding down a towering dune, galloping on horseback towards a massive salt flat – to mellower excursions – observing spurting geysers at dawn, trekking past layercake rock formations at sunset, floating on your back in a crystal-blue laguna – the Atacama is all about outdoor adventure. With so many natural attractions within easy reach of the village of San Pedro de Atacama, the only problem is that you won't have enough time to see and do everything in this dreamlike desert.

THE HAUNTINGLY DESOLATE ROAD TO LAGUNAS ALTIPLANICAS UNDER A THREATENING SKY

Current craze

2014 drew a string of A-list celebrities to the Atacama – including movie stars Antonio Banderas and Juliette Binoche – for the filming of *The 33*, based on the true story of the ordeal and rescue of the 33 Chilean miners trapped underground. Shot partly in Copiapó near the site of the real-life events in the San José mine, the film is set for release at the start of the year.

Trending topic

Until recently, the staggeringly huge mine at Chuquicamata ('Chuqui') was the world's largest producer of copper. It's also famous as a hotbed of social issues: the 2004 Che Guevara biopic *The Motorcycle Diaries* depicts the young revolutionary's visit to the mine – and the way his outrage over poor working conditions helped to shape his political views. Today, it's a side trip from San Pedro that's extremely popular with international visitors.

Most bizarre sight

The 4am wake-up call is worth it when you're standing at the edge of El Tatio, an otherworldly geyser field ringed with volcanoes, at dawn – the sight of swirling pillars of steam against the stark blue backdrop of the altiplano is unforgettable.

Regional flavours

Hiking, cycling, sandboarding, horseback riding – visitors to the Atacama usually work up a ravenous appetite. Classic Chilean comfort foods from empanadas to *pastel de papas* (potato casserole) are on offer at overpriced-for-tourists restaurants in town. Catering more to locals are a handful of restaurants and outdoor food stalls featuring regional specialities like *pataska* (a hearty corn-based stew with vegetables and meat). At night, look for the *rica rica sour*, a delicious twist on the pisco sour made with an aromatic herb that's native to the desert. ● *By Bridget Gleeson*

THE NARROW STREETS OF
HISTORIC MACAU PENINSULA
BUSTLE WITH SHOPPERS
AND RESTAURANT-GOERS

Macau, China

Macau has grown into a mélange of new world glamour and old world grit – and 2015 promises to be a banner year for the region

ACTIVITIES | CULTURE | FOOD

Population **607,500**

Foreign visitors per year **3.94 million**

Languages: official **Mandarin Chinese and Portuguese;** *unofficial* **Cantonese, Patuá**

Major industries **gaming, tourism**

Unit of currency **Macau pataca (MOP$), Hong Kong dollar (HK$)**

Cost index **hotel per night MOP$1500 (US$188), Portuguese dinner for two incl. wine MOP$800 (US$100), taxi from Macau Peninsula to Cotai Strip MOP$150 (US$18.80), ticket to a show MOP$1000 (US$125)**

10

Why go in 2015? > *Glitzy boomtown with cultural mix*

Macau has grown out of its rep as a Las Vegas knock-off and into a mélange of new world glamour and old world grit. With six times more revenue from gaming than Las Vegas, Macau has seen a huge boom in recent years. Nouveau riche mainland Chinese have begun to flock here to enjoy the buzz of China's gambling hub.

But the casino culture belies Macau's true charms. Its Portuguese heritage has created a fusion cuisine that combines European, African, Indian and Chinese elements. And where else in the world can you make an incense offering at an ancient Chinese Buddhist temple in the morning, take the world's highest bungee jump in the afternoon, have a Michelin-starred meal in the evening topped off with a bottle of Portuguese vino, don your finest for a glitzy show and then pull up a plastic stool for some Chinese street food as a midnight snack?

With a spiffy new light rail system connecting the peninsula and islands in the works, as well as major hotel brands like Ritz Carlton and JW Marriott arriving and a slew of new glam casinos under construction, 2015 promises to be a banner year for Macau. And the completion of the world's longest sea bridge between Macau, Hong Kong and mainland China means it'll be easier than ever to get here.

Life-changing experiences

Exploring the back streets of Macau's Unesco World Heritage old town – a mix of Portuguese and Chinese architecture found nowhere else on earth. Sampling the delights of Macanese cuisine, which mixes elements of Portuguese, African and Chinese food – think prawn, chorizo and olive-laden 'Portuguese fried rice'. Thrill-seekers shouldn't leave without a leap off the world's highest commercial bungee platform or a cool stroll around the 233-metre-high Skywalk at Macau Tower.

Trending topic

Space-limited Macau is expanding at an incredible rate, with the Cotai Strip landfill having closed the formerly aquatic gap between Taipa and Coloane and more reclaimed land surfacing by the day. Real-estate prices are soaring, but pressure remains on local businesses to maintain Macau's historic (read: low-rise) architecture. Added to that are ongoing discussions about the democratic process in the lead-up to the 20th anniversary of the region's handover from Portuguese to Chinese sovereignty.

Random facts

■ Macau is the world's most densely populated territory, with more than 21,000 people per square kilometre.
■ At 980,000m², the Venetian Macau is the world's largest casino.
■ According to the CIA, Macau has the second highest life expectancy in the world at 84.41 years.

Most bizarre sight

The golden facade of the Grand Lisboa casino, with its surreal pointed leaves designed to look like a lotus flower, dominates Macau's skyline. And these days, dozens of cranes surround Macau, dredging sand and soil in the middle of the sea to form reclaimed land plots.

Local lingo

Code-switching is a common fact of life in Macau. On any visit, you're likely to hear a local changing seamlessly from Cantonese to Portuguese, English and

THE VENETIAN MACAU, COMPLETE WITH CANALS AND GONDOLIERS, IS THE LARGEST CASINO IN THE WORLD

During the A-Ma Festival, celebrate the Taoist goddess who gave Macau its name ('A-Ma gao' means A-Ma Bay) on 11 May with offerings at her namesake temple and performances of Chinese opera.

As its name would suggest, Macau's rowdiest to-do is the Drunken Dragon Festival on 20 June, when inebriated fishermen parade through the streets waving wooden dragons.

Stretching for an unbelievable five weeks throughout September and October, teams from around the world descend on Macau for the World Cup of pyrotechnic arts, the Macau International Fireworks Competition.

In November, the Macau Grand Prix sees champion motorcycle and race-car drivers take to the peninsula's Guia Circuit, culminating in the Formula 3 Grand Prix race.

Mandarin, though you'll be lucky to hear the local creole, an endangered language known as Patuá.

Regional flavours

With such a mix of influences on its cuisine, the food itself is a reason to visit Macau. Portuguese fried rice, African chicken and charcoal roasted seafood are staple dishes. Another local speciality is the Macanese egg tart – not unlike a Portuguese *pastel de nata*, but made with less sugar to suit local Chinese tastes. Cantonese cooking is also excellent here, from gourmet dim sum to late night *chǎomiàn* from street stalls. And the sweet lack of import tax also means a gorgeous bottle of Douro wine is a no-brainer at most meals.

● *By Megan Eaves*

Macau's Unesco World Heritage old town boasts a mix of Portuguese and Chinese architecture found nowhere else on earth

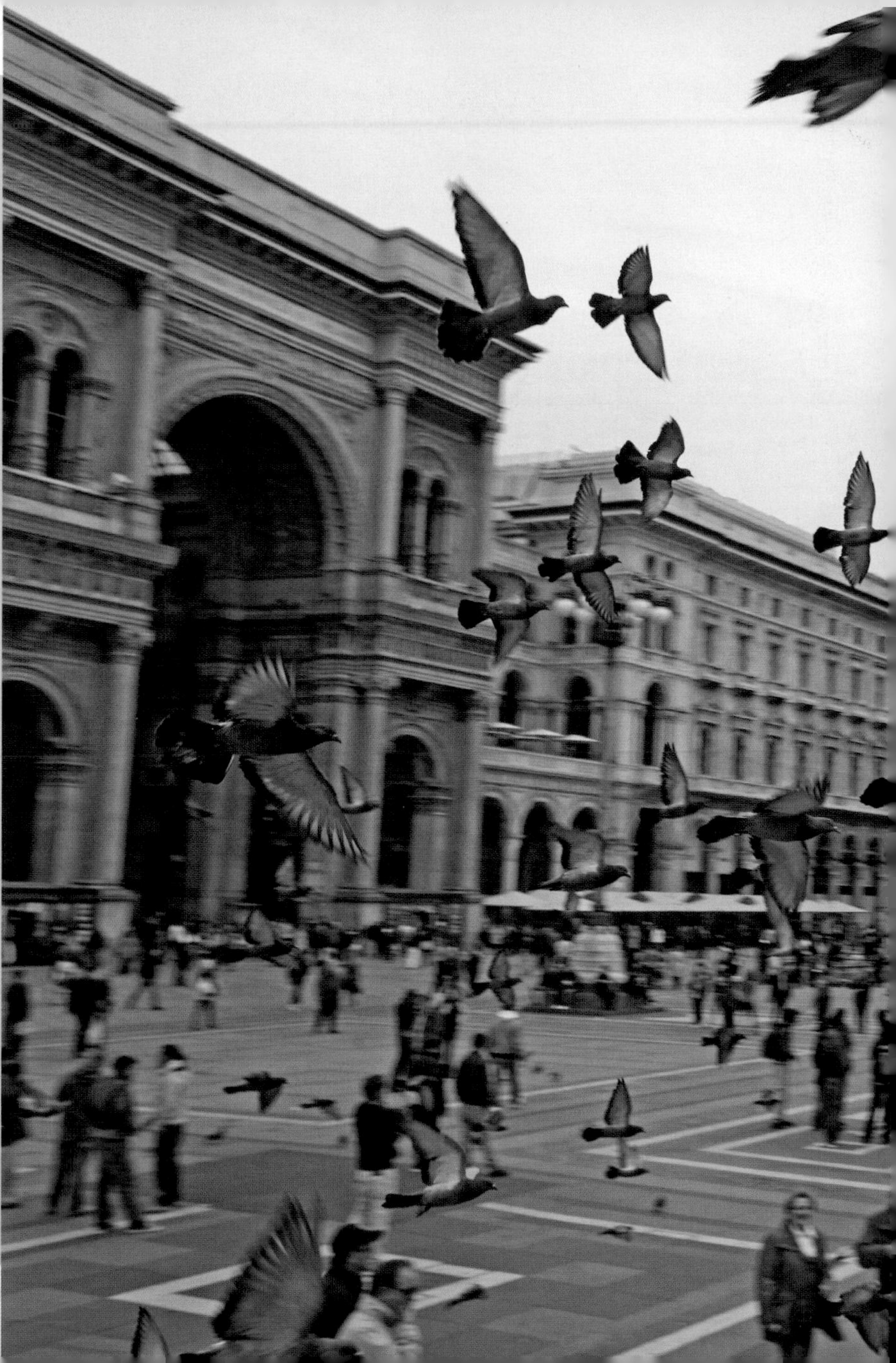

Lonely Planet's Top Ten Cities

THE CAPITOL
BUILDING, SEEN
FROM PENNSYLVANIA
AVE, PRESIDES OVER
WASHINGTON, DC AT DUSK

Washington, DC, USA

The 150th anniversary of Abraham Lincoln's assassination will be marked with the kind of pomp you'd expect from a city whose official religion is national politics

EVENTS | CULTURE | FAMILY

Population **5.8 million**
Foreign visitors per year **1.8 million**
Language **English**
Unit of currency **US dollar (US$)**
Cost index **bottle of wine US$12, hotel (double) for a night US$250, Metrorail Daily Pass US$14, dinner for two (mid-range) US$70**

Why go in 2015? > History in the making

Washington is one of the top museum and monument cities in the world and the Smithsonian Institution, a network of 19 museums, a zoo and several research centres, is a top draw. The 2015 opening of the National Museum of African American History and Culture marks the institution's first new museum in more than a decade. It is the country's only national museum devoted to African-American culture. This year also marks the 150th anniversary of Abraham Lincoln's assassination, which will be marked with the kind of pomp you'd expect from a city whose official religion is national politics and whose history is etched into America's foundation story.

Several mixed-use development projects are in the works – like downtown's CityCenterDC and The Yards, along a formerly industrial stretch of the Anacostia River, both with opening phases throughout 2015 and beyond – with condos, hotels, retail and public outdoor spaces that are transforming the urban landscape and meeting the demands of the city's large population of young professionals. Add to this a vibrant gay bar scene, incredible ethnic eats thanks to thriving immigrant communities (like top-notch Ethiopian) and a venerable performing arts tradition at venues like the Kennedy Center, and the nation's capital is looking more epic than ever.

Life-changing experience

No one would call it uplifting and it's definitely not for younger children, but you will never forget your visit to DC's United States Holocaust Memorial Museum. A powerful monument to the Holocaust, the permanent exhibition spans three floors, tracing an arc from the rise of Nazism beginning in 1933 to the Allied victory in 1945. A display of 4000 shoes of inmates who perished at the Polish Majdanek concentration camp and the Tower of Faces, a high-ceilinged room covered in 1500 photos taken between 1890 and 1941 in the town of Eishyshok (formerly in Poland, now in Lithuania), where over the course of two days in 1941 Nazis and their collaborators eradicated nearly all of the Jewish residents, are especially haunting.

Classic restaurant experience

José Andres, one of America's top chefs and a leading figure in contemporary Spanish cuisine, was born in northern Spain but moved to Washington in the early '90s. Andres may run an empire spanning 13 restaurants (and one food truck) across five cities, but his first-ever restaurant, Jaleo, which turned 20 in 2013, is going stronger than ever. This Penn Quarter favourite is the place to go for classic and contemporary tapas in a setting with as much colour and energy as an Almodovar movie.

Festivals & Events

On New Year's Day 2015 Washington Capitals will host the annual outdoor National Hockey League (NHL) Winter Classic.

14 April 2015 will be the 150th anniversary of the assassination of Abraham Lincoln at Washington's Ford's Theatre by the actor John Wilkes Booth. Ford's Theatre is planning a full commemorative schedule and a replica of Lincoln's funeral train will retrace the original steam engine's trip from DC to Lincoln's hometown of Springfield, Illinois, among other events.

Late March to early April is when the National Cherry Blossom Festival goes off, thanks to the spectacular, ethereal blooms of 3000 trees given to the city by the mayor of Tokyo in 1912. Check the National Park Service's website for 'peak bloom' dates.

No one does Independence Day (4 July) better than the nation's capital. Check out the parade, hit up one of the many block parties and barbecues around the city, then watch the red, white and blue fireworks explode in the night sky.

A FITTING TRIBUTE: THE PORTRAIT GALLERY IN THE HOLOCAUST MEMORIAL MUSEUM

Best shopping

Washington has always been more of a blazers-and-pearls kind of town, but in the last few years the city has experienced a rebirth of style thanks in no small part to a certain First Lady's high-profile designer wardrobe. Georgetown is by far DC's most style-conscious shopping district, with its backdrop of colourful row houses, canal and cobblestones. You'll find everything from finely curated antiques (try Jean Pierre) and designer kids' clothes (The Magic Wardrobe) to unique jewellery (Charm Georgetown).

Classic place to stay

The Willard Hotel (now an InterContinental) traces its illustrious history back to 1850 when brothers Edwin and Henry Willard opened their inn one block from the White House. Having played host to nearly every US president since the mid-19th century and such luminaries as Mark Twain, Charles Dickens and Martin Luther King Jr, the grand dame of Washington hotels has many a tale to tell. Can't afford to spend the night? Stroll through the opulent Beaux-Arts lobby to cocktail hour at the clubby Round Robin bar. Kentucky senator Henry Clay introduced Washington to the mint julep when he mixed one up here in the 1850s and they still use his recipe.

● *By Genevieve Paiement-Jacobson*

A HERD OF WANDERING GUANACOS,
WITH MONTE FITZ ROY RISING
MAJESTICALLY BEYOND THEM

El Chaltén, Argentina

Parque Nacional Los Glaciares, the Hielos Sur Ice Cap – it's no wonder Chaltén has quickly become Argentina's trekking capital. And 2015 is its 30th birthday

ADVENTURE | ACTIVITIES | OFF-ROAD

Population **1000**

Foreign visitors per year **50,000+**

Language **Argentine Spanish**

Unit of currency **Argentine peso (AR$)**

Cost index **970ml bottle of beer AR$15–50 (US$2–6), campsite AR$50–60 (US$6–8), all-you-can-eat** *asado* **AR$100–150 (US$12–20), seven-day guided glacier trek (from US$2000)**

Why go in 2015? > Go before the village grows up

Take a stunningly beautiful Zermatt, raze everything over two storeys (or three stars!), fill it with a motley collection of artisans, entrepreneurs and students, add a *gaucho* or two, then turn a cyclone loose, and you'll be getting close to the vibe of Argentina's newest city.

While the town ('city' is an overstatement) is towered over by jagged 3405m Monte Fitz Roy and enigmatic, ice-rimed Cerro Torre (3102m), its *barrios* include the 726,927 hectares of pristine World Heritage glaciers, peaks, lakes, forests and waterfalls of the Parque Nacional Los Glaciares. Throw in the second-largest chunk of ice outside polar regions, the wild and mysterious

↑

What's Hot...
Long summer days;
hand-crafted beers;
plastic travel gourds for
mate (great for hiking if
you've become addicted
to Argentina's national
drink); coffee socks
(reusable cloth filters,
the best way for a caffeine
hit on the trail)

——

...What's Not
Los vientos (wind).
Screaming in off the
ice cap like a demented
banshee, it will shred
tents, knock over fully
laden trekkers and blow
any loose gear into
Tierra del Fuego.

↓

Hielos Sur (Southern Patagonian Ice Cap), and it's no wonder Chaltén has quickly become Argentina's trekking capital. And 2015 is its 30th birthday!

Even 'town' is optimistic. There's still a village atmosphere, aided and abetted by a straggly main drag, unsealed side roads, lack of mobile phone reception, flakey internet, and a single ATM (which routinely runs out of cash on weekends). The closest airport is three hours away and the only civilised way into town is along Ruta 23 from El Calafate. But this just adds to Chaltén's quirky appeal.

Make no mistake, it's Los Glaciares that people come to see, and there are plenty of trails, views and peaks for enthusiasts of all capabilities, from half-day lakeside meanders to fully tooled week-long sorties out on the ice cap. And if walking or getting vertical doesn't do it for you, consider horseback, mountain bikes, fishing or sucking on a hand-crafted ale among other diversions. Officialdom is refreshingly laid-back.

Life-changing experiences
The snow crunches underfoot as you stop to catch your breath out on the Hielos Sur, a vast expanse of white that stretches mind-bendingly to infinity. Or at least to Chile, where in the distance a range

POCKET-SIZED IT MAY BE, BUT EL CHALTÉN IS UNDENIABLY BIG ON HIGH-OCTANE ADVENTURE

Festivals & Events

Commemorating the first Argentine ascent of Fitz Roy, the annual **Fiesta Nacional del Trekking** in March sees numerous cross-country endurance events held in the surrounding hills.

Desafío Chaltén (Chaltén Challenge) every April combines mountain biking with trekking in an adventure racing team event.

Trending topic

Mobile phone access. Should it come or not? Will it be the end of business or the end of the world? Everyone in town has an opinion.

Classic restaurant experience

Vegetarians stop reading now. After days on the trail eating dehydrated soups and two-minute noodles, there is one dining experience in town that shouldn't be missed, one whose mere mention brings saliva to jaded tastebuds. The all-you-can-eat *asado*. Argentines do barbecue meat with a religious fervour, and the *asado*, complete with charcoal firepit and crucified whole carcasses, is a meat-lover's nirvana. Well, until the day after, when you decide to eat salad for the next week. Look for a tin shed north of Relinchos with the words 'all you can eat' and *'parilla'* outside, but really, any *parilla* (grill) will do.

Classic place to stay

It's busy, cramped and sometimes downright uncomfortable, but there's no greater (nor cheaper) melting pot of travellers than Camping Relincho. Perched above the Río de las Vueltas, campers seek shelter behind trees, fences, cars, anything vaguely out of the wind. Your next-door neighbours could be a pair of hard-core Slovenian climbers, a well-groomed Buenos Aires family spanning three generations, or a lone Aussie motorbiker. When the wind is blowing a gale and your tent is bending double, the warm, cheery, chaotic communal kitchen is a *refugio* in every sense of the word, and somehow, everyone still manages to charge their mobile phones, even though they can't use them.

● *By Steve Waters*

of *nunatuks* (exposed peaks) look like smashed pavlova. Shackleton eat your heart out!

Sit in the cold above Laguna Los Tres watching the first rays of dawn turn the sheer east face of Fitz Roy into molten lava.

Walk into town using the Chilean back door, via Lago O'Higgins and Laguna del Desierto, a multi-day wilderness crossing that sees only a handful of travellers.

The first après-trek beer, a long-neck Quilmes Bock scoffed outside *el supermercado*. You haven't even taken your pack off.

VIA SAN
MAURILIO
IN MILAN'S
CITY CENTRE

Milan, Italy

Expo 2015 – the latest of the world fairs that have been held since the mid-1800s – will be held between May and October, bringing droves of visitors to Milan

CULTURE   FOOD   FAMILY

Population **1.3 million**
Foreign visitors per year **2 million**
Language **Italian**
Unit of currency **Euro (€)**
Cost index **espresso at Café Zucca €5 (US$7), double room in Navigli district boutique hotel from €70 (US$97),** *cotoletta alla milanese* **(breaded veal cutlet) at top-end restaurant €26 (US$36), gem essence facial treatment at Bulgari Spa €130 (US$180)**
Favourite labels **Prada, Dolce & Gabbana, Armani, Missoni, Moschino, Versace**

Why go in 2015?
> *An excellent expo of food, drink and culture*

Milan is a city of lavish wealth and almost frightening elegance. Think bankers in bespoke shoes that cost more than your computer, wealthy *donnas* with Prada handbags and professionally blow-dried hair, elderly ladies walking toy poodles down the Via della Spiga. It's all very pretty to look at, but it can make a mere mortal feel a bit dowdy and down-at-the-heels.

But in 2015, the city will welcome the hoi polloi with open arms. Expo 2015 – the latest of the world fairs that have been held since the mid-

Festival & Events

In early April, MiArt, one of Europe's most important contemporary art shows, draws artists and collectors to buy, sell and schmooze.

Held in April, the Salone Internazionale del Mobile (International Furniture Fair) is the largest event of its kind in the world. Expect parties, events, and tons of drool-worthy (and pricey!) modern furniture.

On 7 December, the charmingly named Oh Bej! Oh Bej! ('so nice, so nice' in the Milanese dialect) is Milan's biggest Christmas fair. Stock up on crafts, goodies and artisanal products of all sorts.

1800s – will be held between May and October, bringing droves of visitors to Italy's second-largest city. This Expo will focus on food – a topic close to any Italian's heart – specifically issues surrounding sustainable agriculture and global nutrition. The 1.1 million sq metre fairgrounds will be laid out like a classical Roman city, with symmetrical avenues, a canal, and a huge artificial lake surrounded by pavilions. Explore the 'future food district', watch cooking demos, wander a plaza full of street musicians and dance performers, or indulge in nighttime wine-tastings. At least 144 countries will participate. In years past, world fairs have introduced or popularised such now-ubiquitous foodstuffs as cotton candy, ice-cream cones and

hamburgers. So come to Milan to find out what we'll all be eating in 50 years.

Life-changing experience

As frilly as a fairy-tale wedding dress, the Duomo di Milano is the world's fifth-largest cathedral. This Gothic marble vision has 135 spires reaching skyward, 3200 elaborately carved statues, ancient and enormous panes of stained glass, and an early Christian crypt containing the remains of St Carlo Borromeo in a rock-crystal casket. The church took some six centuries to complete; be sure to dedicate at least half a day to taking in its glory. Don't miss the roof, especially on a clear day, when you can see the Alps towering in the distance.

What's Hot...

'Ethical fashion' with organic and cruelty-free materials; BikeMI, the city's bike-share program; the Navigli neighbourhood; a classic cappuccino for breakfast

---

...What's Not

Big hair and bling; crashing that cute Vespa you don't know how to drive; overdressing for La Scala (no tuxes, please); ordering a cappuccino after lunch

IT WOULDN'T BE MILAN WITHOUT RETAIL THERAPY: SHOP 'TIL YOU DROP AT GALLERIA VITTORIO EMANUELE II

So you're shopping in Milan's elegant, glass-vaulted Galleria Vittorio Emanuele II when you notice a well-dressed man or woman doing something... odd

Trending topics

Italy is mad for coffee – the nation gulps some 14 billion cups of espresso each year. Milan alone has 600 cafes, where baristas grind, measure and pour with the precision of scientists and the vision of artists. So why, then, would Italy need Starbucks? That's the question on many a Milanese tongue as rumours fly that the Seattle-based megachain is looking to open in Italy in the near future. Could the classic cappuccino soon be a Frapuccino? Stay tuned.

Most bizarre sight

So you're shopping in Milan's elegant, glass-vaulted Galleria Vittorio Emanuele II when you notice a well-dressed man or woman doing something... odd. Standing in front of the 19th-century bull mosaic on the floor, they place their right heel on the bull's testicles and rotate three times. This bizarre tradition of unknown origin is said to bring good luck. Not so for the bull – years of fortune seekers have worn a hole in his manhood.

Classic restaurant experience

The breaded veal cutlets known as 'veal Milanese' in much of the world are *cotoletta alla milanese* here in the city of their birth. For the crispiest, juiciest, most golden butter-fried *cotoletta* in town, take a taxi to the city's old meat district, where cosy Trattoria del Nuovo Macello has been battering and frying cutlets since 1928.

● *By Emily Matchar*

SAVE YOUR LEGS
AND HOP ON THE
MOUNTAIN RAILWAY
NEAR ZERMATT'S
ICONIC MATTERHORN

Zermatt, Switzerland

In 2015 this swish Swiss diva of mountain resorts revs up its legendary party spirit to celebrate the 150th anniversary of the first ascent of its magic mountain

ACTIVITIES ADVENTURE FAMILY

Population **5670**
Foreign visitors per year **1.08 million**
Language **German (the Swiss version that no one actually writes)**
Unit of currency **Swiss franc (Sfr)**
Cost index **cup of coffee/Walliser beer Sfr4/5 (US$4.51/5.65), hotel double/dorm room Sfr130–800/40 (US$145–900/$45), one-day ski pass Sfr75 (US$84.74), a glass of champagne at 3883m Sfr15 (US$16.95)**

4

Why go in 2015? > Anniversary attitude at altitude

When it comes to hardcore attitude at altitude, Zermatt takes no prisoners. Since the end of the 19th century intrepid hikers, mountaineers and ski fiends have drooled like soppy, love-struck kittens over the god-of-a-mountain Matterhorn that rises above the town in spellbinding pyramidal perfection.

But never more so than in 2015, when this swish Swiss diva of mountain resorts revs up its legendary party spirit to celebrate the 150th anniversary of the first ascent of its magic mountain. English mountaineer Edward Whymper triumphantly led his party of seven to the summit of the 4478m-high Matterhorn on 14 July 1865 – only for him and three others to crash 1200m to their deaths down the North Wall after their rope broke on the descent. The bittersweet tragedy ushered in the meteoric rise of Zermatt as one of the hottest high-altitude spots on earth.

Anniversary action includes the July opening of Hörnli Hut, a mountain hut perched with one finger to the gods at 3260m, at the base of the Matterhorn. Inside this brand-new building – architectural homage to the sun with all the sustainable-energy whistles and knobs on – world-class alpinists take refuge before dicing with death on the final iconic ascent up sheer rock and ice.

No sweat if you're not superhuman or even a climber: nail-biting theatre recreating Whymper's historic ascent (and disastrous descent) will take to the open-air stage in Zermatt town. The backdrop? *Au naturel* of course darling – and as effortlessly sensational as you would expect from this seductive natural beauty of a town: the mountain itself!

> **Alpine action defines Zermatt. Give your ski legs a run for their money down the highest slopes in the Alps**

Life-changing experiences

Alpine action defines Zermatt. Give your ski legs a run for their money down the highest slopes in the Alps. Melt over Matterhorn views along ski-virgin blues, marvel at the mountain's unfathomable trigonometry from long, scenic reds and scare yourself to death on knuckle-whitening blacks. Die-hards only please on Zermatt's serial killer Triftji, one of the toughest mogul runs known to man.

Festivals & Events

Alpine hipsters, this is your chance to see how the big boys do it. Ski touring has never been so hot and even the world's ski touring elite will break out in a sweat during Matterhorn Ultraks Skialp on 11 April. The summertime trail run of the two-part alpine race follows on 22 August.

Zermatt Unplugged from 14 to 18 April brings five days of unadulterated acoustic music into town. The 2015 line-up in the festival marquee and club stages promises to be extra star-spangled.

A party like no other takes over on 14 July 2015, the official day of celebrations for the 150th anniversary of the first ascent of the Matterhorn.

Ride the Matterhorn Glacier Paradise, Europe's highest cable car, up to 3883m and gawp at a top-of-the-beanstalk panorama of 14 glaciers and 38 mountain peaks over 4000m. Not bad, Zermatt, not bad at all.

Chase the sunrise or moonlight with old-fashioned finesse aboard Zermatt's romantic, 19th-century cogwheel railway (another 'Europe's highest' tick on the scoreboard) to Gornergrat. Try not to be struck dumb by the mind-blowing view when you alight at 3089m.

ZERMATT'S MIND-BLOWING ALPINE VIEWS AND WORLD-CLASS SKIING MAY PROVE HARD TO RESIST

↑

What's Hot...
Tickets for summer
theatre performances
of the first Matterhorn
ascent

What's Not...
Cars with combustion
engines, last season's
skiwear (ie, any ski
garment not sufficiently
hip to double as
streetwear)

↓

Trending topic

Even world darling Zermatt is not immune to glacial melt. If global warming continues apace, glaciers in Zermatt and the surrounding Valais region could shrink by up to 90% by 2100.

Most bizarre sight

Few museums in the world boast a tatty, broken old rope as their star attraction: Zermatt's Matterhorn Museum does.

Classic restaurant experience

It has been on the celebrity hobnobbing circuit for decades but remains as black-book chic as the day it debuted. But there again, what is there not to like about dining al fresco on organic air-dried meats at a century-old farmhouse, snug in a soft fleecy blanket amid full Dolby surround of soaring mountain peaks and the Matterhorn. Chez Vrony is the name. ● *By Nicola Williams*

THE SUN SETS OVER
VALLETTA'S ANCIENT
MARSAMXETT HARBOUR

Valletta, Malta

The Maltese capital has had a sensational makeover. Perhaps it's to do with coming up to a big birthday. At almost 450 years old, Valletta could be accused of going through a mid-life crisis

CULTURE | EVENTS | FAMILY

Population **199,000**
Foreign visitors per year **1 million**
Languages **Maltese, English, Italian**
Unit of currency **euro (€)**
Cost index **cup of coffee €1 (US$1.40), hotel double for a night from €30 (US$40), short taxi ride €10 (US$14),** *pastizz* **(traditional pastry) €0.30 (US$0.40)**

Why go in 2015? > 450 years since the great siege

You haven't been to Valletta? If not, this oversight must be righted. As soon as possible. Thankfully you're timing it right: the Maltese capital has had a sensational makeover.

Perhaps it's to do with coming up to a big birthday. At almost 450 years old, Valletta could be accused of going through a mid-life crisis. Over the past few years, it's had a thorough overhaul, with architectural botox aplenty, not all of it to the local taste. The injection of contemporary architecture includes Renzo Piano's graceful new gateway to the city, the Italian architect's parliament building, faced with laser-cut stonework, and his open-air auditorium, a metal

Valletta was built and decorated during the 17th century, and celebrates its all-out baroqueness via the International Baroque Festival, centred on the ornate Manuel Theatre and St John's Cathedral for the second half of January.

The Valletta Jazz Festival is held in July against the backdrop of Valletta's Grand Harbour, with international and local artists jamming and playing every type of jazz, from flamenco fusion to traditional.

During Birgu by Candlelight in October, the tiny city of Birgu across the harbour is lined with candles, so that the beautiful narrow streets are entirely flame-lit.

A COLOURFUL JUMBLE OF MALTESE BALCONIES ON REPUBLIC STREET, VALLETTA

> **Valletta has stayed remarkably trim, with its unspoilt 17th-century buildings lining a beautifully laid-out grid of streets**

skeleton built atop the Opera House ruins.

This tiny capital is limited by geography, sitting as it does on a small, almost-island peninsula, so it's never had the facility to sprawl inelegantly outwards. Valletta has thus stayed remarkably trim, with its unspoilt 17th-century buildings lining a beautifully laid-out grid of streets, at the end of which you can glimpse the cobalt sea. The contrast between the old and the new is what makes Renzo Piano's new additions all the more startling. Visit and make up your own mind.

But the other reason that you should visit this

year is that the city will commemorate 450 years since the Great Siege. In 1565, a paltry number of Maltese Christian knights battled an army of marauding Turks, with much carnage, dirty tricks and bloodshed on both sides. This remembrance will be particularly strong on 8 September, National Day, which is preceded by a special mass and literary evening the previous night.

Life-changing experiences

Rich in museums, Valletta centres on one of the most fabulously decorated baroque cathedrals you are ever likely to see, St John's Co-Cathedral, whose interior is a frenzy of decoration, a product of the Knights of Malta all trying to outdo each others' chapels. It also houses Caravaggio's largest painting.

Don't leave without seeing a performance in the new open-air theatre, which rises, phoenix-like, from the ruins of the 19th-century opera house that was bombed in WWII.

Also make sure you take a boat trip around the harbour and a wander around the streets of Birgu (also known as Vittoriosa). This small town, the original Knights of Malta headquarters, has stunning views across to the capital that eclipsed it.

Current craze

The Grassy Hopper sells healthy, organic vegan and vegetarian food. Their first outpost was a van on Ta'Xbiex waterfront and they've now opened an outlet on Old Theatre St. Not only is the food delicious, healthy and inventive, but they donate leftover food to the YMCA to feed the homeless several days per week.

Trending topic

What do you think of the Renzo Piano additions to the Valletta cityscape? Many Maltese are angry: they think the buildings are ugly, and they're fuming that they cost so much money to build when everyone's been asked to tighten their belts.

Random facts

■ Malta suffered 154 continuous days and nights of bombing during WWII (by contrast, London suffered 57).

■ The British king George VI awarded the George Cross award for bravery to the entire population of Malta after WWII.

■ Malta and its seas frequently stand in as film locations, with recent shoots here including *Game of Thrones*.

Most bizarre sight

Among the National Museum of Archaeology's most treasured exhibits are some perky prehistoric stone phalluses.

Classic restaurant experience

The backstreet, old-school, unfussy ambience of Trattoria da Pippo means that dishes here are served with lashings of atmosphere. You'll eat hearty Italian-influenced Maltese cuisine amid a hubbub of local clientele: a place for those in the know. Lunch only. ● *By Abigail Blasi*

A SNOWY PLOVDIV GLOWS
BRIGHTLY AS DUSK FALLS
OVER THE CITY

Plovdiv, Bulgaria

Plovdiv has emerged from its colourful all charming cobblestoned streets, delicately painted houses, craft markets, quirky museums and temptingly affordable shopping

CULTURE | FOOD | VALUE

Population **339,000**
Language **Bulgarian**
Unit of currency **lev (lv)**
Cost index **double hotel room 70 lv (US$49), shot of *rakia* 3 lv (US$2), plate of grilled pork and potatoes 10 lv (US$7), gallery or heritage building visit 3 lv (US$2)**

Why go in 2015? > **A gem emerges after eight millennia**

One of Europe's most beautiful Old Towns, with a backdrop of Bulgaria's dramatic Rhodope Mountains. Historical treasures by the thousand. Smouldering nightlife and a wicked sense of humour. There's a wealth of reasons to explore Bulgaria's second city, yet Plovdiv has always flown under the radar.

Recent decades have polished Plovdiv into a spirited modern city, without ever dulling the glint in its eye. Its remarkable ruins (including an amphitheatre right in the centre of Plovdiv's main shopping precinct) were slowly excavated throughout the 1970s and '80s. In 1990 the long awaited sports complex

(Bulgaria's largest) was finally completed. And throughout the 2000s, heritage buildings left to gather dust under Communism have been lovingly restored into museums, restaurants and hotels. At long last Plovdiv has emerged from its cocoon: all charming cobblestoned streets, delicately painted houses, craft markets, quirky museums and temptingly affordable shopping. And it's been well worth the wait.

Life-changing experiences

Like the 'Eternal City' of Rome, Plovdiv is made up of seven hills. But Rome is a fresh-faced youngster compared to Plovdiv, one of Europe's oldest cities. Plovdiv is thought to date as far back as 6000 BC. The city's turbulent transformation from Neolithic settlement to Thracian fortress, and its transition from Roman to Byzantine to Ottoman rule, can be traced through Plovdiv's 200 archaeological sites and beautifully preserved buildings (don't miss the splendid Djumaya mosque).

But the city's most delightful neighbourhood was born out of the Bulgarian Revival of the 18th and 19th centuries. The Old Town, a jewellery box of timbered houses and church spires, glows in shades from duck egg blue to warm turmeric.

Festivals & Events

From late May to mid-July Plovdiv bursts into life with music, performing arts and historical commemorations for the Cultural Month Festival.

Opera lovers will delight in June's Verdi Festival when twilight performances take place in the Roman amphitheatre.

Embrace music and nature at the Meadows in the Mountains Festival, also in June, set in the Rhodope Mountains.

Visit in late July to early August to shake your embroidered skirts at Plovdiv's International Folklore Festival.

There's free entry to every gallery in Plovdiv during the Night of the Galleries in September.

What's Hot...
Local artists; student activism; repurposed buildings; bohemian cocktail bars

...What's Not
Crumbling Soviet blocks

Once your cultural appetite is sated, let the Rhodope Mountains lure you beyond the city

ASEN'S FORTRESS IN THE RHODOPE MOUNTAINS DATES FROM THE 12TH CENTURY

Colourful landmarks like St Nedelya's bell tower form an eye-boggling contrast against Brutalist creations like the central post office and the twisted metal helix of the Main Square fountain.

Once your cultural appetite is sated, let the Rhodope Mountains lure you beyond the city. Explore Asen's Fortress, a Thracian outpost perched above jagged valleys, or seek serenity at Bachkovo Monastery.

Current craze

Plovdiv has some of Europe's most distinctive public art. Check out the striking Balkan murals inside the Ethnographic Museum's garden walls, or the Cubist mural blazing out where ulitsa Saborna meets ulitsa Krivolak I. Look out for cheeky street art like caricatured electricity boxes too.

Random fact

■ French poet Alphonse de Lamartine paused in Plovdiv after an epic 'voyage in the Orient' in 1833. Locals were utterly beguiled by their literary guest and to this day commemorative plaques beam out from the house he slept in. Former French president Mitterrand even came to pay it a visit in the 1980s.

Most bizarre sight

'Miljo the Crazy' was a fixture of Plovdiv's eccentric cast of characters, spreading joy (and exasperation) with his eavesdropping and pranks. Locals couldn't bear to think of a world without Miljo's antics so they kept him around in the form of a gurning statue in the main shopping precinct.

Classic restaurant experience

Carnivores will be spoilt for choice in Plovdiv, but Puldin Restaurant – a stone-walled cellar bedecked with Roman artefacts – is an enchanting backdrop to savouring grilled meats. Kick-start your meal with a shot of ice-cold *rakia*, best served with a *shopska* salad of cucumber, tomato and slivers of sheep's cheese.

Best shopping

For an enticing array of unguents and fragrances featuring Bulgaria's famous rose oil, head to Refan on ulitsa Knyaz Alexander I. Another unmissable souvenir is Troyan pottery, bowls and tableware painted with distinctive swirls and droplets – find some of the most dazzling examples along ulitsa Saborna. For locally made jewellery, clothing and quirky souvenirs, browse the open-air fair outside the Ethnographic Museum.

● *By Anita Isalska*

SALISBURY CATHEDRAL, SEEN FROM THE WATER MEADOWS THROUGH THE EARLY MORNING MIST

Salisbury, UK

2015 is set to be the year visitors linger in this quintessentially English city as Salisbury uncorks the champagne for the 800th anniversary of its greatest treasure, the Magna Carta

CULTURE | EVENTS | FOOD

Population **45,000**
Foreign visitors per year **1 million**
Language **English**
Unit of currency **Pound sterling (£)**
Cost index **pint of local ale £3.60 (US$5.90), double room £85 (US$140), afternoon tea with scones and cream £15 (US$24.70), cathedral tower tour £10 (US$16.50)**

Why go in 2015?
> *Celebrate Magna Carta's 800th anniversary*

For too long travellers have considered Salisbury a short stop on the way to Stonehenge. But 2015 is set to be the year visitors linger in this quintessentially English city as Salisbury uncorks the champagne for the 800th anniversary of its greatest treasure, the Magna Carta.

It would be hard to underestimate the impact of the 'Great Charter'. Sworn and sealed on the banks of the Thames in 1215, the Magna Carta limited royal power and established the rights of common people. It became a bedrock of English law and inspired movements for justice and freedom worldwide.

The eighth centenary of this iconic parchment is igniting revelry across England – folk opera, calypso tributes and 13th-century ale-brewing have all been mooted as ways to mark the occasion. As home to the best-preserved original copy (the others are in London's British Library and Lincoln Castle), Salisbury will be leading the charge.

The lightning rod for the celebrations will be Salisbury Cathedral, the neck-straining medieval masterpiece whose Chapter House holds the Magna Carta. The cathedral itself boasts a clutch of superlatives, with the tallest spire in Britain, the world's oldest working clock and Britain's largest cloister.

A brand new exhibition will launch in the Chapter House, alongside an array of talks, evensongs, a flower festival and plenty more still being planned. It's hard to imagine a more inspiring time to visit Salisbury than a year when the streets will be alive celebrating man's universal freedom.

Life-changing experiences

Recall the days of wimpled maidens and warring kings by exploring the city's medieval sights, starting with the stone-carved Poultry Cross in the market square. A gilded lion and unicorn still glower down from the coat of arms crowning the North Gate, a stone archway thought to date to 1327. And the dark of heart won't want to miss the Gothic Church of St Thomas Becket, harbouring

> *Old Sarum isn't simply an ancient fort, it's also a place where adrenaline junkies can skydive or soar in small aircraft*

apocalyptic murals that still elicit a thrill of fear.

Who could conceive of bypassing the pubs? Salisbury's nightlife has Purple Flag status, issued to impeccably polite and welcoming cities – an awfully British award, if ever there was one. Drink in views over the River Avon at the Old Mill, or bask in old-time ambiance at The Cloisters. Sup local ciders and ales (try Three Daggers) but look out for local wines too (a'Beckett's Vineyard produces some very quaffable drops).

Current craze

Old Sarum isn't simply an ancient fort, it's also a place where adrenaline junkies can skydive or soar in small aircraft. Propeller-heads can also get their fix from the ground at the Boscombe Down Aviation Collection.

Random facts

■ Wiltshire locals are nicknamed 'moonrakers', dating from when smugglers hid contraband in local ponds, fishing it out by night. If questioned, they'd claim to be raking the moon's reflection to get cheese.

AN AERIAL VIEW OF OLD SARUM'S ANCIENT RUINS – NOW A HOTSPOT FOR THRILLSEEKERS LOOKING FOR KICKS

Festivals & Events

Special events will be taking place throughout 2015 to celebrate the Magna Carta – check the Visit Wiltshire (www.visitwiltshire. co.uk) and Salisbury Cathedral (www. salisbury cathedral. org.uk) websites for the latest.

Enjoy two smouldering weeks of contemporary sculpture, photography and installations at the Salisbury International Arts Festival, starting 23 May (www. salisburyfestival. co.uk).

See Salisbury in bloom during Magna Flora, the enormous week-long flower festival planned for September 2015.

■ Are Salisbury's historic properties rousing déjà vu? You may have seen them on screen. Stately Mompesson House was a film location for 1995's *Sense and Sensibility*.

■ If you stumble leaving the pub, blame the local ghosts rather than an excess of ale. Several sites in Salisbury are thought to be haunted, from pubs to crossroads to Debenhams department store.

Most bizarre sight

Crop circles appear near Salisbury every summer and the phenomenon is eagerly discussed in the local Crop Circle Information and Co-ordination Centre. Just look out for those little green men.

Classic restaurant experience

You need not fear an empty belly in a region with a constellation of Michelin-starred restaurants and excellent pub food. For something truly special, family-run Charter 1227 restaurant serves up lip-smacking and locally sourced British cuisine. Think suckling pork belly that melts on the tongue, guinea fowl and unapologetically indulgent parfaits and terrines. ● *By Anita Isalska*

THE ROCOCO GREAT GALLERY IN THE PALACE OF SCHÖNBRUNN FEATURES CEILING FRESCOS BY ITALIAN ARTIST GREGORIO GUGLIELMI

Vienna, Austria

In 1865 the last significant Hapsburg monarch got cracking on his architectural tour de force: the Ringstrasse. 150 years later, the 'Ring' is still its showpiece

CULTURE   EVENTS   FOOD

Population **1.7 million**
Foreign visitors per year **5.8 million**
Language **German, with a relaxed Viennese accent**
Unit of currency **euro (€)**
Cost index **coffee and cake at a Kaffeehaus €6–9 (US$8–12.50), wurst at sidewalk stand €3.50 (US$5), tram/U-Bahn ticket €2.10 (US$3), high profile museum €12–14 (US$16–19)**

8

Why go in 2015? > Ring in the new

If you like it then you should put a ring on it. Emperor Franz Josef didn't need Beyoncé to tell him that. In 1865 the last significant Hapsburg monarch got cracking on his architectural tour de force: the Ringstrasse. The boulevard to outpomp them all, the 'Ring' made a lavish embrace of Vienna's historic centre, stitching together trophy sights from the Gothic-revival Rathaus to the neo-Renaissance wedding cake that is the Staatsoper. It was bold. It was grand. It was wincingly expensive. And it changed the face of Vienna to such an extent that, 150 years later, the 'Ring' is still its showpiece. In 2015, a line-up of special events and exhibitions is

Festivals & Events

Waltz, foxtrot and polonaise with the best of Vienna's carefully coiffed, nimble-footed socialites at one of the city's 450 balls in January and February, which swing from queer to kitsch. The Opera Ball (12 February 2015) is the jewel in the crown.

Click into the groove of summertime Vienna at the Donauinselfest in late June. Bands rock the Danube Island with free gigs attracting a crowd of three million.

Vienna goes snow-globe for December's fairy-tale Christmas markets (head to those at Rathausplatz, Schönbrunn and Altes AKH), then rings in the New Year with its world-famous concert at the Golden Hall.

> *This is a city where you can go clubbing in your dirndl, talk opera at the sausage stand and live out your very own 21st-century fairy-tale*

VIENNA'S KUNSTHISTORISCHES (ART HISTORY) MUSEUM STANDS ON THE FAMOUS RINGSTRASSE

cranking up the celebratory feel.

You want more gravitas? The University of Vienna is turning 650 in 2015. Sigmund Freud, Anton Bruckner and 15 Nobel prize winners will be forever associated with this, the oldest university in the German-speaking world. A guided tour of its arcades, chambers and library affords more insight.

Vienna didn't grab the number-one slot in Mercer's 2014 Quality of Living survey by merely resting on its historic laurels, however. The city of strudel and Strauss can also innovate and steal the limelight – be it with contemporary art in born-again bread factories or Kim Kardashian dangling off the arm of billionaire Richard Lugner at the Opernball. Forget compromises and social

boundaries this is a city where you can go clubbing in your dirndl, talk opera at the sausage stand and live out your very own 21st-century fairy-tale. And as the shiny new Hauptbahnhof reaches completion in 2015, arriving in the Austrian capital has never been easier. Go to Vienna. Go now. You'll have a ball.

Life-changing experiences

Oh, Vienna! Whether you cram in the culture or do sweet nothing in a coffee house, this city will win you over in its inimitable fashion. After all, where else can you dip into the murky world of psychoanalysis (Sigmund Freud Museum), drift through parks where Mozart once dallied (Burggarten), and watch white Lipizzaners perform equine ballet (Hofburg)? The Austrian Empire encrusted its capital with palaces to swoon over like Unesco listed Schönbrunn, and squirreled away a never-ending supply of art masterpieces, not least the ultimate embrace – Klimt's *The Kiss* at the Upper Belvedere. Ride high in the Riesenrad (Giant Ferris Wheel) of *Third Man* fame to see Vienna flutter like a pocket handkerchief below you.

Current craze

Something old becomes something new. Buoyed by the success of ventures like Haus des Meeres (an aquarium in a defunct WWII flak tower) and the Pratersauna (poolside electro and techno in a former sauna), Vienna is still gleefully waving its reinvention wand. Favourites? Puff, a brothel turned retro-cool cocktail bar on Gumpendorferstrasse, and the Ankerbrotfabrik in the 10th district, Europe's biggest industrial bread factory reborn as a contemporary art and design gallery space.

Classic restaurant experience

Embedded in the greenery of the Stadtpark and lodged in a former dairy, the Meierei (sister of two-Michelin-starred Steirereck) is the real deal for Viennese classics. The kitchen elevates breakfast and brunch to the extraordinary, with dishes like scrambled ostrich eggs and Alpine beef tartare. Or pop in for the best goulash in town, coffee and cake or the 120-variety cheese board.

Best shopping

Fledgling designers spread their wings in the 7th district's backstreets, where boutiques sell everything from streetwear with indie edge to vintage silk numbers and handmade jewellery. Ina Kent's versatile bags and the folksy-Fräulein-meets-21st-century-sex-kitten styles of catwalk queens Lena Hoschek and Susanne Biovsky are all the rage. For deli delights, foraged herbs and home-spun fashion, go off-piste in the Freihausviertel, which spreads south of Vienna's famous food-market mile, Naschmarkt.

Most unusual place to stay

The decentralised, hotel-as-home approach of Urbanauts Street Lofts is like a breath of fresh air. With the aim of revitalising local businesses, the Viennese architect trio Kohlmayr, Lutter and Knapp have transformed a sprinkling of empty shops and tailors' workshops into sleek, super-stylish studios. There's everything you need to tap into the neighbourhood – from insider tips on coffee houses, hammams and cool nearby bars to movies and free bicycle rental.

● *By Kerry Christiani*

MARVEL AT CHENNAI'S
JAW-DROPPING
KAPALEESHWARAR TEMPLE

Chennai, India

With the opening of the Chennai Metro Rail, the first integrated mass transit system in India, Chennai plans to raise its profile on the international stage

Population **4.4 million**
Foreign visitors per year **3.5 million**
Language **Tamil**
Major industries **automobiles, IT, finance**
Unit of currency **rupee (Rs)**
Cost index **cup of chai Rs8 (US$0.13), masala dosa Rs15–50 (US$0.25–0.83), double hotel room per night Rs500–2000 (US$8.30–33.30)**

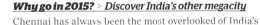

Why go in 2015? > Discover India's other megacity

Chennai has always been the most overlooked of India's megacities. While travellers rave about Delhi, Mumbai and Kolkata, the capital of India's steamy south has long been seen as a stepping-stone to other parts of India, rather than somewhere to visit on its own merits. Ask the average person to name the most famous sight in Chennai and many would struggle to reply.

Locals hope to change all that in 2015. With the opening of the Chennai Metro Rail, the first integrated mass transit system in India, Chennai plans to raise its profile on the international stage and earn a reputation as more

than just a jumping-off point for 'more interesting' places nearby. If nothing else, the fast and frequent air-conditioned trains will certainly transform the experience of exploring this hot and humid metropolis.

And there's plenty to see: statue-covered Dravidian temples, institutes for Indian classical dance, fascinating museums, British-era fortifications and churches, a 3km-long beach that throngs with locals night and day, and India's second-largest movie industry, centred on 'Kollywood' in the western suburb of Kodambakkam.

Life-changing experience

Strolling on Marina Beach is the quintessential Chennai experience. This broad strip of sand is where Chennai comes to unwind, and early evening is prime time to promenade, go jogging, play beach cricket, fly a kite, catch a fish, buy a giant balloon, munch on street food, swim (fully clothed, of course), or just sit on the sand looking out at the Bay of Bengal. OK, it's not Waikiki, but the frenetic beachside activity offers a mesmerising window onto the rhythms of the Indian south.

Current craze

Breaking records – Chennaites have got the bug for record-breaking stunts, and the city has garnered many laurels in recent years, including the awards for the longest continuous drumming session (50 hours) and the largest group

Festivals & Events

Cows are in seventh heaven for Pongal (14 to 17 January in 2015), when treats made from rice and cane sugar are offered to all and sundry, including any sacred bovines in the vicinity.

In March or April, locals flock to Mylapore's Kapaleeshwarar Temple to witness the annual parade of Lord Shiva and family during the energetic Arubathu Moovar festival.

Psychedelically coloured statues of Ganesh are ritually immersed in wells, tanks, ponds, rivers and the ocean for the Vinayaka Chaturthi festival, which falls on 17 September in 2015.

There's plenty to see: statue-covered Dravidian temples, institutes for Indian classical dance, fascinating museums, British-era fortifications and churches

of people playing keyboards together at one time (229). Who knows what 2015 will bring?

Trending topic

The lives, loves and larger-than-life screen personas of Tamil film stars. Enjoyed by an estimated 77 million Tamils across the globe, the films produced in Kodambakkam take the social mediasphere by storm, as locals debate the latest hits, flops, dance routines, romances, love triangles, marriages and separations of the big Kollywood stars.

Random facts

■ The city changed its name from Madras to Chennai in 1996 as part of a national process of de-Anglicisation, but both terms were British abbreviations for the names of local villages.

■ Chennai is known as the Detroit of India thanks to its prolific automobile industry, producing 40% of India's cars.

■ Chennai sits on the thermal equator, meaning the climate is as hot, hot, hot as the city's famously spicy south Indian curries.

Most bizarre sight

Probably the tomb of St Thomas the Apostle, reputedly killed on St Thomas Mount in Chennai in AD 72 while spreading the Christian message in southern India, just 14 centuries earlier than the 'official' arrival of Christianity with the Portuguese in 1498. Whether Thomas the Apostle really died in India has never been verified, but locals have venerated the site since at least Roman times, according to the writings of ancient scribes.

Classic restaurant experience

No starched white tablecloths here – Chennai's finest food is served on a banana leaf in a humble Tamil canteen. The first branch of Hotel Saravana Bhavan was out in the Chennai suburbs, but the cooking was so spectacular that branches sprang up across the city, then across the country, then across the world. At any branch, locals queue round the block at lunchtime for stunningly spiced *thalis* (plate meals), *dosas* (rice-flour pancakes) and south Indian snacks, all served with the secret-recipe house *sambar* (tamarind sauce). ● *By Joe Bindloss*

MYPALORE FESTIVAL'S POPULAR KOLAM CONTEST, IN WHICH PARTICIPANTS PAINT GEOMETRIC PATTERNS ON THE STREET IN CHALK

CONQUER THE DIZZYING
HEIGHTS OF TORONTO'S
CN TOWER EDGEWALK

Toronto, Canada

The most multicultural city in the world promises to be extra vibrant in 2015, when an estimated 250,000 visitors arrive for the Pan American (Pan Am) Games

FOOD | CULTURE | EVENTS

Population **5.2 million**
Visitors per year **21 million**
Languages **English, French**
Unit of currency **Canadian dollar (C$)**
Cost index **hotel per night C$70–450 (US$63–407), TTC (subway) ride C$3 (US$2.70), CN Tower admission C$32 (US$29), Toronto Island ferry C$7 (US$6.30)**

Why go in 2015? > Spectator central...

The most multicultural city in the world, a bustling megalopolis where over 140 languages are spoken, promises to be extra vibrant in 2015, when an estimated 250,000 visitors arrive for the Pan American (Pan Am) Games. A bunch of public works projects have advanced in preparation for the C$1.5 billion international multisport games, including the long-anticipated Union Pearson Express train, which will whizz passengers from the airport to downtown in 25 minutes, making it easier than ever to sink one's teeth into the culinary and cultural delights of Toronto's diverse enclaves.

Ubiquitous condo towers, aging megahighways and the lack of a unifying architectural theme aren't likely to seduce you, but the character and flavour of Toronto's neighbourhoods just might. Expect 2015 to be another massive year for Toronto's drool-worthy restaurant scene. If nightlife is your bag, you'll love this city: the influences of nearby New York and Montreal keep things cutting-edge. Live music thrives in gritty, grassroots bars and band-rooms.

Life-changing experiences

Get a sense of the bigger picture atop Toronto's beloved CN Tower, and brave the tethered but hands-and-barrier-free Edgewalk around the roof of the main observation deck (356m), if you dare. Hop on a ferry to Toronto Island for a sunny afternoon stroll and the best views of the

↑

What's Hot...

Ossington Ave (West), Danforth Ave (East), Porter Airlines, Evergreen Brick Works community environmental centre, Royal Ontario Museum, Waupoos peach cider

—

What's Not...

Mayor Rob Ford, winter, potholes, TTC delays, downtown and highway traffic, hipsters, poutine

↓

TORONTO'S SKYLINE AT NIGHT, VIEWED FROM TORONTO ISLAND

Festivals & Events

In June, rock on for North by Northeast's 21st birthday in this week-long extravaganza of live music, performance and film in bars and venues across the city.

Pride week also takes place in June. Toronto revels in its status as one of the world's most gay-friendly cities, culminating in the mile-long Pride Parade.

Luminato, also in June, sees a delectable selection of the planet's top performers across all genres descend upon Toronto for this series of public concerts. Some are outdoors; many are free.

In 2015, Toronto plays host to the Pan Am Games (10 to 26 July) and Parapan Am Games (7 to 15 August). Surpassed in participation only by the Olympic and Commonwealth Games, the Pan Ams promise spectators a fortnight of the Americas' best athletes smashing their PB's.

Toronto International Film Festival (TIFF) will take place from 10 to 20 September in 2015. It's the jewel in the crown of Toronto's festival calendar, and one of the biggest in the world film festival circuit.

soaring skyline then zip back to your digs, lose the civvies and dress to impress. Kick off your fabulous evening with an al fresco cocktail at the Terrace at Stock, on the 31st floor of the Trump hotel. For dinner, stroll west on King to Lee Lounge, an Asian-fusion taste explosion, best shared. Once your taste buds have thanked you, the bars and clubs of the Entertainment district (at your feet) and Queen West (a few blocks north) await. Will you dance or rock the night away?

Best shopping

Above Queen and Dundas TTC stations, the giant Eaton Centre mall houses over 230 big-branded retailers. A few blocks north, the 'Mink Mile' west of Yonge St, on Bloor St, is where you'll find Gucci, Prada, Chanel and the folks who can afford them. Funky young things should head immediately to the Queen West and Kensington Market 'hoods for a mother lode of old-school and new-cool boutiques and a massive selection of vintage threads and dreads.

Classic place to stay

Tucked away off Bloor St in downtown's most desirable locale, the Windsor Arms is a 1927 neo-Gothic mansion preferred by visiting glitterati who favour privacy and personal attention over the need to be seen. Luxurious oversized suites are classically styled with modern conveniences – each has a separate bath and shower and every room features a musical instrument: many have been strummed, plucked or tinkled by the Greats.

● *By Benedict Walker*

Lonely Planet's
Top Travel Lists

Best Value Destinations for 2015

Bang for your buck and pizzazz for your pound: here's where to stretch this year's travel budget until it oozes contentment.

1 Tunisia

When it comes to Tunisia, the conversation has moved on from safety to recovery for tourism, and a renewed appreciation of why the country is such a compelling destination. Travel warnings have been dropped and travellers are once again tuning in to North Africa's most compact package. This year prices will remain tempting to lure travellers back, and lower crowds will mean that those who do come will get a more rewarding experience whether they stay in cosmopolitan Tunis, head for Saharan *Star Wars* sets or explore the Roman remains that dot the north of the country.

Seasonal charters from European airports to Djerba can be an excellent-value gateway into Tunisia.

2 South Africa

Currency fluctuations mean that for certain travellers South Africa is more affordable than it has been for many years. Instead of just rejoicing in the undercooked rand, consider what South Africa offers value-seeking travellers at any time. How about fantastically accessible wildlife watching for all budgets, bargain public (and traveller-friendly) transport and free entry to many of the country's museums? Most visitors will find something to please their budget, whether it's a cheap-and-cheerful Cape Town seaside cafe or an affordable safari campsite.

Come in South Africa's shoulder seasons (February, March, September and October) for the best combination of low crowds and comfortable weather.

3 Shanghai

For all the upscale new openings in China's most famous coastal city, Shanghai remains reassuringly affordable for budget travellers. No-nonsense dorms start at less than US$10, and the pleasing pricing continues through budget and mid-range hotels until you hit the less-than-friendly international big names and trendy boutique accommodation. It's a similar story when eating out: characterful street-treats for a dollar, and big portions in popular restaurants for little more. Best of all, walking the city's safe and buzzing streets is the best way to take the pulse of this fast-changing metropolis.

SmartShanghai (www.smartshanghai.com) is a great place to keep pace with new happenings in this ever-changing city.

4 Samoa

It feels like we've heard this one before. 'Beautiful, undeveloped tropical paradise seeks underfunded travellers for discreet liaison. Applicants must enjoy no-nonsense budget buses and simple, idyllic beach hut accommodation (*fales*), owned by local families, who tend to throw in dinner. So as with so many places before it, we'd say get to Samoa soon. Best visited by jumping off from New Zealand or Australia, these islands are one of the best travel deals in the Pacific.

The markets of Apia, Samoa's capital and largest town, offer a great introduction to everyday life. Maketi Fou, the biggest, is the place to come for souvenir hunting and Samoan street food.

Top Travel Lists ● ● ● ● ● ● ●
● ● ● ● ● ●

MEDENINE IN TUNISIA WAS USED AS A SETTING IN THE *STAR WARS* FILMS

5 *Bali*

While many budget-traveller favourites have grown up and got proper jobs running overpriced resorts, Bali never stopped delivering the goods. In fact, while backpacker-friendly beachside bungalows and other affordable digs still abound, with reasonable costs for food and transport thrown in. Bali is also pretty stonking value for mid-range adventurers who delight in air conditioning, distinctive Balinese style and a large range of quality places to stay. And of course, Balinese spa treatments are rightly famous, and cheaper than in many other places.

Bali's international popularity is evidenced by the large number of winter flights from Russian cities – offering the unlikely combination of a snowy Trans-Siberian journey and a week on a Balinese beach.

6 *Uruguay*

While Brazil's travel scene burgeons as the World Cup rolls into town, Uruguay looks a better-value choice for a short excursion into South America. This proud buffer state has much to enjoy: sizzling steaks, laid-back Montevideo and a hip beach scene that tempts travellers further round the sandy coast each year. While you should watch out for peak-time costs on the coast, this remains an underrated, affordable corner of South America. *The sleepy riverside town of Fray Bentos is home to a memorable museum: the former factory of the world-famous beef processor of the same name.*

7 Portugal

That Portugal's Algarve region trumps prices at other European resort areas isn't a surprise to regular visitors. This surf and family-friendly region remains the destination of choice for a more-than-sun seaside holiday, and it's not all that great-value Portugal has to offer. Lisbon (pictured overleaf), as happening as Barcelona with fewer crowds, and cheaper, is set to get a whole lot more accessible as low-cost airline Ryanair opens a base in the Portuguese capital. Head anywhere in the country off the tourist trail, and costs come down further. *For a great-value tour of Lisbon hop on tram 28, which rattles around taking in many of the city's highlights, including the Alfama district and the views from the Miradouro de Santa Luzia for €2.85.*

8 Taiwan

Taiwan delivers great all-round value. Taipei is significantly cheaper than Hong Kong, Seoul or Tokyo, and while hotels are a big expense, dorm beds and homestays abound in Taiwan and camping is common in a lot of the island's national parks and forests. Rail passes are standardised and cheap on fast and modern lines. Admission to many attractions and temples is cheap, and even major museums are affordable. Eating, perhaps the main attraction in Taiwan, is accessible to all whether tucking into dumplings at a street stall or enjoying high-end fare at lower prices than comparable cities. *A large bottle of Taiwanese beer will set you back around NT$120 (US$4), or much less if you get one from a grocery shop.*

9 Romania

Eastern European nations frequently appear in best-value lists, but in Romania's case the entry is entirely warranted. Now vigorously connected to the rest of Europe by budget airlines, accommodation compares well in all price brackets to bigger-name destinations in the region. Bucharest is a case in point, where hotel beds largely welcome business travellers, so holiday season is, unusually, low season. Away from here there are budget-friendly homestays in medieval villages, spectacular castles and the unique Danube Delta, best explored by inexpensive, if slow, ferries. *Private vans known as 'maxitaxis', together with buses and minivans, form the cheapest way to get around Romania. See www.autogari.com for routes, times, fares and departure points.*

10 Burkina Faso

Burkina Faso remains a rare gem. Little known, but producing sighs of wanton desire to return from anyone who's been. Those in the know will tell of colourful markets, friendly locals, spectacular rock formations and the immense fun of Ouagadougou, the tongue-twisting capital with a lively arts scene. With costs affordable and surprisingly good wildlife-spotting in the south you'd be hard-pressed to find a more satisfying introduction to West Africa. *At the top end of travel around Burkina are reliable air-conditioned buses, with guaranteed departures and advance ticketing. At the other are more ramshackle taxi-brousses (bush taxis) which cover more remote stops.* ● *By Tom Hall*

Special Anniversaries in 2015

2015 sees the anniversary of many important events – some poignant, some life-changing, and some of global significance.

1 Magna Carta turns 800, England

The 'Great Charter' was signed by King John at the instigation of his unruly barons at Runnymede on the banks of the Thames in 1215. At the time it was simply an attempt to wrest power from an unpopular monarch and nobody present can have expected its legacy to have endured for eight centuries, but phrases such as 'To no-one will we sell, to no-one deny or defer justice or right' have become enshrined in the legal systems of Britain, the US and beyond, guaranteeing the document continuing fame and importance.
Details of events commemorating the anniversary can be found at magnacarta800th.com.

2 Battle of Waterloo, Belgium

The battle that finally put an end to French Emperor Napoleon's career took place 200 years ago this year. It was on Sunday 18 June 1815 that the man who had dominated France and Europe for over a decade capitulated at Waterloo, in what is now Belgium. The British, under the Duke of Wellington, repeatedly held off French assaults until the Germans, under Blücher, arrived and chased the emperor and his troops from the field. Europe settled down to an unprecedented period of peace. Wellington was so popular at home he became prime minister. And Napoleon was exiled to St Helena where he died in 1821.
The site of the battle can easily be visited from Brussels. The website www.waterloo200.org has details of bicentennial events.

3 Anniversary of the world's first restaurant, France

French cuisine, delicious as it may be, is not considered the healthiest these days, with its generous amounts of cheese and lashings of cream. But 250 years ago, when a Monsieur Boulanger opened the world's first restaurant near the Louvre in Paris, his aim was to sell customers 'restorative' dishes to improve their health. The term 'restaurant' itself comes from the French 'restorer', to restore, and Boulanger's business, on the rue Bailleul, drew the crowds with his soups and broths, starting a culinary trend that the rest of the world embraced wholeheartedly.
Restaurant Boulanger no longer exists but Paris isn't exactly short of decent eating options. For top recommendations check out www.lonelyplanet.com/france/paris/restaurants.

4 Tallest building's fifth birthday, UAE

In a world where new super-skyscrapers are being built on a daily basis, it's a surprise that one building, the Burj Khalifa in Dubai (pictured), has held on to the tallest-building record for five years. Reaching a vertigo-inducing 830m, since opening in 2010, it's seen off contenders for the title with ease (the world's next highest building, the Makkah Clock Royal Tower Hotel in Mecca, is a measly 601m). But its days in the number one spot are numbered, with another Saudi Arabian skyscraper, the Kingdom Tower in Jeddah (1007m) due for completion in 2019.

Plan your visit to the highest point of the manmade world by visiting www.burjkhalifa.ae.

5 Seventy years since first atomic bombs dropped, Japan

As WWII dragged on in the Pacific through 1945, the USA took the decision to use its recently developed atomic bombs to force Japanese capitulation. On 6 August the *Enola Gay* dropped the bomb nicknamed 'Little Boy' on Hiroshima. On 9 August a second bomb was dropped on Nagasaki. On 15 August the Japanese agreed to an unconditional surrender. Up to 250,000 people died in the two bombings, still the only use of atomic weapons in a war scenario. The two cities successfully rebuilt themselves but seventy years on haven't forgotten the destruction they suffered.

Peace memorials in both cities can be visited; see www.pcf.city.hiroshima.jp and www.peace-nagasaki.go.jp for details.

Top Travel Lists ● ● ● ● ● ● ● ● ● ● ● ● ● ● ● ●

6 Quarter of a century since Nelson Mandela freed, South Africa

After spending 18 years imprisoned on tiny Robben Island in Table Bay, just off the coast of Cape Town, Nelson Mandela walked to freedom on 11 February 1990, watched on television by millions of people around the world. After years of political unrest and increasing violence against the apartheid government in South Africa, his release was a massive step, coinciding with the legalisation of all political parties, including his own ANC party, and ultimately leading to the first fully democratic elections in the country four years later.

Today the island is open to visitors with the website www.robben-island.org.za providing information.

> **After spending 18 years imprisoned on tiny Robben Island in Table Bay, just off the coast of Cape Town, Nelson Mandela walked to freedom on 11 February 1990**

7 American Civil War ended 150 years ago, USA

After four years of conflict, the end of the American Civil War, which had split the country and killed around 750,000 soldiers and civilians, was finally in sight when General Lee surrendered his Confederate army on 9 April 1865 in Appomattox Court House. Lee's act was just the first step in the end of the war, triggering a chain of similar surrenders across the south, most too late for the Union president, Lincoln, to see – he was assassinated five days after Lee's surrender in Ford's Theatre, Washington. It wasn't until 23 June that the last Confederate general, Stand Watie, gave up.

From Fort Sumter in South Carolina where the first battle took place, to Appomattox Court House, there are many war sites that can be visited today (www.nps.gov/civilwar).

8 The Lord of the Rings turns 60

Having taken him a painstaking 12 years to write, Tolkien's epic fantasy, *The Lord of the Rings*, was finally published in full in October 1955, when the last volume, *The Return of the King*, was released. Urged by his publishers to produce a sequel to his hugely popular *The Hobbit*, Tolkien wrote what has become the second-biggest selling novel of all time, with over 150 million copies sold. The story of Frodo and his quest to destroy the all-powerful One Ring has been the inspiration for countless other fantasy novels and the source material for one of the most popular film franchises in movie history.

New Zealand, where the movies were made, has attracted millions of tourists wanting to follow in Frodo's large footsteps. Check out www.newzealand.com/int/feature/lord-of-the-rings to plan your own trip to Middle-earth.

9 Cunard celebrates 175 years

It was back in 1840 that Samuel Cunard began operating the first scheduled UK–North America boat service, kick-starting the age of the ocean liner. The *Britannia* was the first ship to make the crossing, sailing from Liverpool on 4 July and arriving in Halifax, Canada, 12 days later. Facilities for the 115 passengers aboard included a ladies-only saloon, and the fare of 34 guineas covered 'provisions and wine'. Charles Dickens didn't enjoy his trip on the *Britannia* in 1842 but he was in a minority as Cunard's and its rivals' success throughout the rest of the century would show.

For more on the anniversary, or to book a place on the commemorative sailing, go to www.cunard.co.uk.

10 Eighty years of Aya Sofya museum, Turkey

Of course Aya Sofya is older than 80 but it was in February 1935 that Istanbul's most popular sight and one of the world's architectural masterpieces became a museum. It was Turkish leader Ataturk who, as part of his Westernising policies, changed the building's purpose from religious to secular. From its construction in AD 537 until the Ottoman conquest of Byzantium in 1453, Aya Sofya had been a cathedral and centre of Greek Orthodox Christianity. It was then a mosque for the next four and a half centuries before opening as, arguably, the world's most beautiful museum 80 years ago this year.

Head to www.ayasofyamuzesi.gov.tr/en for information on visiting the museum.
● *By Cliff Wilkinson*

EXPLORE THE DIMINUTIVE SET-PIECE VILLAGE OF HOBBITON IN NEW ZEALAND, WHERE THE LORD OF THE RINGS MOVIES WERE FILMED

Top Travel Lists ● ● ● ● ● ● ● ● ●

Unforgettable Family Travel Experiences

Inspire a sense of wonderment in the next generation with our best family travel activities.

will awaken future Attenboroughs and seeing these almost-mythical creatures of many a bedtime story in the flesh (elephants, rhinos, buffaloes, lions and leopards) will leave you with indelible memories. With accommodation from camping to luxury lodges suiting any budget and family's needs, you really can do an African wildlife-spotting safari this year.

The best time to visit is May to October, when wildlife congregate around diminishing waterholes.

1 Self-drive safari, Namibia

Etosha National Park, with its otherworldly landscapes and the Big Five in their natural habitat (not to mention 340 bird species, including the greater flamingo), is accessible in an ordinary sedan on a family self-drive safari from Windhoek. A few nights in this lauded wildlife sanctuary

2 British Museum treasure hunt, London, UK

For kids, traipsing around a museum doesn't cut it in the new world of electronic media and instant access to the world's online resources. But there are still opportunities to wow youngsters at a museum, literally stuffed full of rarities from across the globe. The British Museum is not alone in doing a sterling job of making history accessible for kids, creating treasure hunts and activities to

guide younger ones through the best of their collections. Even better: join one of their free hands-on activities and share the fun of learning by making your own comic-book version of ancient Mayan history or Viking helmets for the whole family.
Download floor plans and pre-plan your visit at www.britishmuseum. org; entry is free.

3 Sailing the Whitsundays, Australia

Crystal clear waters and white beaches fringe the forested domes of these 'drowned mountains' where you can sail in calm seas protected from the ocean by the Great Barrier Reef. Camp in secluded bays and swim and snorkel among colourful marine life while you island-hop through the archipelago. For the novice a crewed charter may be best, but almost anyone can learn to skipper a sailing boat with a little training provided by the bareboat charter companies. Only seven islands have resorts here, the rest are uninhabited and waiting for you to explore.
Budget A$1000 a day for a party of six. Some crewed packages offer diving too. See www. tourismwhitsundays.com.au for more.

4 Ancient rock art, Dordogne, France

Ignite archaeological imaginations by learning about ancient rock art in France. Petroglyphs are pretty cool whatever your age, from youngsters who are just grasping how old the world may be, to your street-art-loving teen. The most famous here are the paintings of the Grotte de Lascaux, where Cro-Magnon artists depict a whole menagerie including mammoths, horses, ibex, reindeer, aurochs and bulls. The gallery at Rouffignac is also one of the world's oldest, and most beautiful. There is now speculation that these multicoloured frescoes signed off with haunting handprints may have been painted by the womenfolk of the clan between 15,000 BC and 10,000 BC.
Find out more about touring the picture-perfect villages and food culture of the region at www. northofthedordogne.com.

Top Travel ● ● ● ● ● ● ● ● ●
Lists ● ● ● ● ● ● ● ● ●

5 Horse riding expedition, Wyoming, USA

A slower and more engaged way to experience mountain wilderness, clopping along mountain trails by horseback (pictured overleaf) is a must for anyone craving a new frontier in family activities. See mountains blooming with wildflowers, rivers flowing with trout, and moose, elk or deer grazing in meadows. There are plenty of options depending on your comfort level, from riding out to a dude ranch camp where fishing and hiking are also on the agenda, to taking a guided stock trip into the backcountry of Yellowstone National Park. The valley may be packed with tourists in summer, but get off the beaten track and you'll leave 95% of them behind you. *Find details of tours at www. wyomingtourism.org/thingstodo/ listings/Horseback-Riding-Guides/1405945. Roads can be closed in winter so check ahead.*

6 Elephant sanctuary, Sukothai, Thailand

Thailand has so much to offer travellers, but for families wanting something especially memorable, spending time volunteering at Boon Lott's Elephant Sanctuary will inspire and educate. The complexity of human and animal competition for land and resources, and how we relate to the animal kingdom at an up-close-and-personal level, are among the learnings your children will take home from here. Accommodation is in basic cabins with cold-water showers, so this is not for the soft touch. But paying to stay also helps fund their mission to 'protect, expand and educate' with the local community in the Sukhothai hills. *Book ahead as the project is popular. Information on how to get there and what to bring can be found at www.blesele.org.*

7 Harry Potter at Disney World, Orlando, USA

You've read the entire Harry Potter series together – now you can play-act your way around the Disney World version of the make-believe land of Hogwarts. Half the time here you'll be reminiscing about your first terrifying rollercoaster ride as a kid, the rest will see you planning your Disney trip on a map, allowing only a brief refuelling pit-stop for lunch. The Wizarding World of Harry Potter ticks every family-holiday box, the first being: magical. *Park tickets cost around US$400 for a family of four. The experience is also open at Japan's Universal Studios.*

8 Snorkelling with stingrays, Cayman Islands

The extensive marine-park system of the three Cayman islands provide numerous launch spots to snorkel together among neon fish and rainbow-coral gardens. And off Grand Cayman congregate huge, fearless stingrays, sliding up to suck morsels of squid directly from the hands of humans at Stingray City. Meet your new best friend, the prehistoric ray. Some may question the ethics of feeding these fish directly, but no one doubts the experience is truly exhilarating. Surprisingly, its popularity only enhances this experience: with more punters and more rays it's a feeding frenzy at dinner-time in the shallows.

Note: friendly stingrays are still deadly marine animals, this isn't a risk-free activity. See www.caymanislands.co.uk/activities/attractions/stingraycity.aspx.

9 Canopy zip line, Sacsara Valley, Peru

This one's for adventurous parents who now have children. Strap yourself on to a flying fox and whizz between mountains for a shared experience in terror and triumph that your kids won't ever forget.

Cola de Mono Canopy zip line stretches high above the spectacular scenery of the Sacsara Valley. Apparently in six years of operation there hasn't been an accident and the equipment is absolutely strong enough to carry you with your child (who must be over six) in tandem across a gorge. The outfit also runs kayaking and rafting trips on the Santa Teresa river for families with older children.

A prepatory course takes about two hours, and camping accommodation is provided back at base (www.canopyperu.com)

Blanketed in snow, the moorlands and mountains of Norway turn into a wintery wonderland that you can criss-cross with light-weight skis

10 Cross-country skiing, Norway

Blanketed in snow, the moorlands and mountains of Norway turn into a wintery wonderland that you can criss-cross with light-weight skis on specially prepared tracks (pictured above). The Peer Gynt Trail, named after the folkloric Norwegian, is best for families, with ski lodges at regular intervals. Cross-country skiing is free, you just need to organise ski-hire and accommodation. However, first-timers may prefer to tackle this on a tour which includes instruction, a guide and luggage transfers. The Norwegians have a very clear mountain code to follow ensuring no one puts themselves in danger. *Weather conditions can change quickly so never venture out without a map. The trail also makes for pleasant hiking in summer. See www.visitnorway.com/en/product/?pid=125813.*

● *By Tasmin Waby*

Best Places to get a Yes

Once you've chosen to spend the rest of your life with that special someone, you're faced with what can feel like an even greater decision. Where do I pop the question?

1 Bagan, Myanmar (Burma)

Sunrises are inherently romantic, but those in Bagan are truly surreal. The capital of the Kingdom of Pagan between the 9th and 13th centuries, Bagan was once blessed with 10,000 Buddhist monasteries, temples and pagodas. Today, the plain around Bagan is still dotted with more than 2000 of them. Climb to the top of one together (Lawkaoushaung is a great choice) and watch the rising sun turn the dark landscape into a vivid golden canvas eloquently brushed with silhouettes. It's an incredible sight to witness, and it's a perfect time to pop the question.

The best time to visit Bagan, located 118 miles south of Mandalay, is between November and February.

2 Trolltunga, Skjeggedal, Norway

If she loves the great outdoors, isn't scared of heights and is willing to walk to the edge of the world with you, she'll certainly overlook the fact you dropped to one knee on something called 'The Troll's Tongue'. The most epic of natural settings, Trolltunga is a dramatic sliver of rock that extends precipitously over a 700m abyss and overlooks the lake of Ringedalsvatnet far below. Come well prepared as this is a remote mountain environment. the return hike from the trailhead takes eight to 10 hours.
Trolltunga is typically accessible from mid-June (after the snow melts) to mid-September. Bergen is the nearest major city.

3 New York City, USA

Full of romantic locations, New York City is a justifiable favourite for proposals. Some sites even help you to go the extra mile: the Rockefeller Center's outdoor skating rink offers you exclusive ice time and will play a CD of your choice, and the Empire State Building's famous 86th-floor observation deck has a saxophonist who takes requests. Another lofty location with iconic city views, but none of the hype, is the footpath on the Brooklyn Bridge. In summer, Central Park's Loeb Boathouse is an inspired choice – rent a paddle boat for two, hire a gondola or propose while dining on the lakeside terrace.
Empire State Building tickets cost US$27, while exclusive access to Rockefeller rink is US$350. Details about Loeb Boathouse are found at www.thecentralparkboathouse.com.

Top Travel Lists ● ● ● ◉ ● ● ○ ○
● ● ● ● ● ● ● ○

4 NamibRand Nature Reserve, Namibia

In the Namib Desert you don't need moonlight to strike the mood, the stars are bright enough on their own. The NamibRand Nature Reserve is one of only three gold-rated International Dark Sky Reserves in the world. After spending a wonderful day enjoying the area's dunes, mountains and abundant wildlife, you'll be tempted to propose at sunset (it is breathtakingly beautiful), but hold off until the celestial fireworks are in full flow. *The NamibRand Nature Reserve is found in Namibia's southwest and can be accessed by road or by chartered light aircraft; for more details visit www.namibrand.org.*

5 Amalfi Coast, Italy

Yes, Venice, Rome and Florence are all great choices, but the Amalfi Coast south of Naples is meant for couples in love. There are some rather remarkable spots to ask the all-important question, such as the lofty Terrace of Infinity at Villa Cimbrone (pictured overleaf) in Revello or the Sentieri degli Dei (Path of Gods) high above Positano. But the Amalfi Coast is the kind of place where you'll likely find the perfect spot of your very own. *Villa Cimbrone's garden and Terrace of Infinity is open daily from 9am to sunset; entry €7. For more details visit www.villacimbrone.com.*

A HOT-AIR BALLOON RIDE OVER BAGAN HAS A ROMANCE ALL OF ITS OWN

6 Udaipur, Rajasthan, India

The Rajasthani city of Udaipur was dubbed 'the most romantic spot on the continent of India' in 1829 by Colonel James Tod, the first political agent in the region for the East India Company. Its ornate palaces, temples and havelis straddle the shore of Lake Pichola and the white-marble Lake Palace seemingly floats on the lake's gentle waters. Now a luxury hotel, it is a storybook setting for an engagement.
Rooms at the Taj Lake Palace start from £219 per night; for more details visit www.tajhotels.com.

7 Arches National Park, Utah, USA

Displaying the power, fragility and beauty of both nature and time, the red rock formations of this national park are an inspirational engagement setting for couples who love exploring the outdoors together. Delicate Arch, with the La Sal Mountains as a backdrop, is one of the most captivating outcrops. Double O Arch and the Double Arch are rather intimate spots too. If you are both into rock climbing or mountain biking, this area of eastern Utah will give you even more to celebrate.
Arches National Park, 6km north of Moab, is open year-round; entrance is US$5, campsites are US$20. Visit www.nps.gov/arch for more information.

8 Paris, France

Paris, the City of Light, is mesmerisingly beautiful and remains one of the world's most romantic cities. The Pont des Arts pedestrian bridge that spans the Seine near the Louvre is an atmospheric option for a marriage proposal – its surroundings are sublime. A more understated, but incredibly charming idea is to propose on one of the picturesque iron footbridges over the tree-lined Canal Saint-Martin in the 10ᵗʰ arrondissement.
Spring and summer are gorgeous, but more expensive and crowded. Autumn and winter in Paris have their bright spots too, with lovely decorations and far fewer visitors.

9 Príncipe Island, São Tomé and Príncipe

Where? Exactly. Finding a paradisiacal island in a country that few people have ever heard of will score you points for creativity, and Príncipe's deserted beaches and gorgeous tropical backdrop make for a truly intimate and special engagement. Located off the west coast of Africa in the Gulf of Guinea, this petite nation has a very casual and peaceful vibe, something you'll quickly (and happily) sink into.
The best time to visit is June to September. Bom Bom Island Resort is the ideal place to stay; for more information visit www.bombomprincipe.com.

10 Antarctica

A destination of majestic proportions, Antarctica has the power to overwhelm. During the long voyage across the vast empty Southern Ocean, you'll truly understand that Antarctica is not just a remote part of the world, but the end of it. In the days that follow, you'll also discover that this cold and hostile environment is hauntingly beautiful. Add a little warmth with your love (and a diamond doesn't hurt!) and you have makings for an almighty 'YES!'
The best time to visit is November to March; at the height of summer, there is up to 20 hours of sunlight a day. ● *By Matt Phillips*

The Best Free Things to do in 2015

Travel doesn't have to break the bank: here's our guide to the best travel experiences that – like love – don't cost a thing.

and Albert Museum, dedicated to five thousand years of fashion and design, from Persian carpet weaving to the post-punk street wear of Vivienne Westwood. Best of all, admission to all three Kensington museums is free, though the V&A gift shop in particular will test your frugal resolve.

A tunnel links South Kensington tube to the Kensington museums, but walk above ground for lunch stops on Exhibition Rd.

1 The Kensington Museums, London, UK

Welcome to Kensington, home to well-heeled lords and ladies, chauffeur-driven Rolls Royces, and London's favourite free museums. The Kensington museums are London's cultural triumvirate: specimens collected by Charles Darwin grace the collection at the Natural History Museum, while the world's first steam train sets the pace at the Science Museum. Then there's the elegant Victoria

2 Star gazing in the desert, Nevada, USA

You haven't seen sparkle until you've seen the night sky over the desert. Once you escape the light pollution pulsing out of Las Vegas, the skies above Nevada provide spectacular opportunities for star gazing. Desert trails near the former gold-rush township of Tonopah offer views onto an uninterrupted starscape, with a remote chance of spotting secret test aircraft and maybe even UFOs from nearby

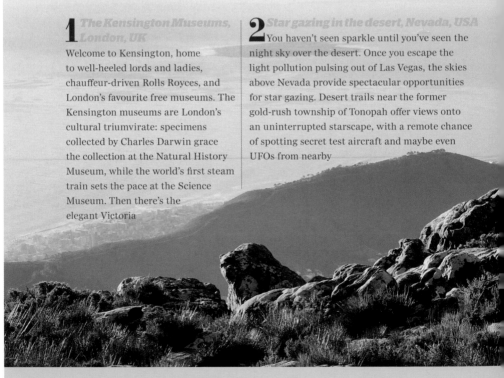

Groom Lake, aka Area 51. If ET fails to appear, you'll still be rewarded by the sight of 7000-plus stars and the clear outline of the Milky Way.

The historic Mizpah Hotel (www. mizpahhotel.net) offers visitors to Tonopah a taste of the pioneer spirit; at least one bed has wagon wheels!

3 Lunch at the Golden Temple, Amritsar, India

They say there's no such thing as a free lunch, but admission – and meals – are complimentary at the Golden Temple in Amritsar. Hospitality is one of the core tenets of the Sikh religion, and every day an estimated 40,000 pilgrims file into the Guru-ka-Langar, the vast, hangar-like temple canteen, for a simple meal of chapattis, vegetable curries and rice. All are welcome to join the dinner queue after completing a ritual circumnavigation of the Amrit Sarovar, the 'Lake of Nectar' surrounding the Golden Temple, but a donation is appropriate to help the charitable work of the temple foundation.

As well as eating at the Golden Temple, you can stay in the niwas *(pilgrims hostels) – see www.goldentempleamritsar.org.*

4 Rock al Parque, Bogotá, Colombia

Tired of paying Beverly Hills prices for rock festivals in muddy fields? Then look no further than Rock al Parque in Bogotá, Colombia. You'll still find the muddy fields and dubious toilets, but the ticket price is a cool zero pesos. Latin America's three-day premier showcase for rock talent serves up everything from twiddly speed metal and power-chord stadium rock to punk, blues and ska. The Dead Kennedys appeared in 2011, so you know the festival has credibility. But a word of warning, – alcohol, smoking and metal belts are banned inside the venues.

The main venue for Rock Al Parque, is Simón Bolívar Park; check out the upcoming line-up at www.rockalparque.gov.co (in Spanish).

Top Travel Lists ● ● ● ● ● ● ● ● ● ● ● ● ● ●

5 Trek up Table Mountain, Cape Town, South Africa

Planet Earth has plenty of dramatic viewpoints, most with a price tag as stratospheric as the views. Not so Table Mountain (pictured overleaf). Those willing to brave the gruelling trek from Cape Town to the summit can enjoy one of Africa's most iconic views for free, with the fall-back option of the cable car for the trip back to town. Armed with drinking water and protection from the elements, you can choose from some 350 trails that force their way up the rocky cliffs, or play it safe on the India Venster route, following the path of the cable car to the peak.
A map is essential if you hope to conquer Table Mountain – locals rate the maps produced by Peter Slingsby (www.slingsbymaps.com).

> **Every year from late autumn to early spring, the aurora borealis repaints the night in hypnotic, impressionist colours**

6 Relax on the beach in Rio de Janeiro, Brazil

When Rio de Janeiro needs to let its hair down, it heads to the beach. The sandy strips at Copacabana, Ipanema, Leme, Leblon and Barra da Tijuca are a playground for surfers, beach volleyball teams, sun-worshippers, guitar players, and beautiful people just strutting their stuff. Bring a few bills for a beer at a beachfront kiosk and the rest is free. As part of the build-up to the 2016 Olympics, free wi-fi is provided along the most popular beaches, but most locals leave valuables behind so they can plunge into the ocean at a moment's notice.
Inexpensive public buses ply the coast; routes 583 and 584 serve Copacabana and Ipanema.

7 Admire the Northern Lights, Lapland, Finland

The price of a hotdog and beer might make you wonder how anywhere in Scandinavia could make it onto a list of the world's top free experiences, but the experience in question is served up for all to see in the winter sky. Every year from late autumn to early spring, the aurora borealis repaints the night in hypnotic, impressionist colours, which pulse even more vividly once you cross the Arctic Circle. Lapland is a favourite vantage point, especially on the icy shores of Lake Inari, homeland of Finland's Sami people.
Inari lies on the bus route between Ivalo and Rovaniemi, both served by flights from Helsinki.

8 Ride the Staten Island Ferry, New York City, USA

You can't say you've seen New York until you've seen New York from the Staten Island Ferry. Cruising from St George on Staten Island to Whitehall in Lower Manhattan, this fare-free commute offers the same first glimpses of America that greeted thousands of new settlers after processing on Ellis Island. The undisputed highlight is the toe-to-torch view of the Statue of Liberty, but the approach to Whitehall terminal, with its backdrop of iconic skyscrapers, comes a close second.
Ferries run at least hourly in both directions, 24 hours a day – see www.siferry.com for schedules.

THE GOLDEN TEMPLE'S
FREE LUNCH OFFERS
WONDERFUL PEOPLE-
WATCHING OPPORTUNITIES

9 Surf it up in Sydney, Australia

Free experiences are in short supply in Australia's most expensive metropolis, but if you provide the board, the surf is gratis. Sydney's famous surf beaches are open to all, and that includes such legendary breaks as Manly, Curl Curl, Dee Why, Narrabeen and Freshwater, where Hawaiian legend Duke Kahanamoku pioneered the sport in 1914. Travellers looking for a cheap way to board-up will find stacks of used boards in local op-shops (second-hand stores) along the coast. If surfing isn't you thing you could always take a free dip in the Dee Why Rockpools or the Bronte or Freshwater Baths. *Surfboards can be carried free on Sydney city buses and trains, so long as you don't block the way for other passengers.*

10 See the Symphony of Lights, Hong Kong, China

The illuminated skyline of Hong Kong is one of the world's great spectacles. Factor in the Symphony of Lights, staged every night from 8pm, from the buildings on the harbour and you move from spectacle to spectacular. Fireworks add to the show on special occasions such as Chinese New Year. The best vantage points for this optical overload are Tsim Sha Tsui waterfront, the Golden Bauhinia Square promenade in Wan Chai, and the ferries that criss-cross Victoria Harbour. *A sound show accompanies the lights at Tsim Sha Tsui waterfront and Golden Bauhinia Square, with commentary in English on Monday, Wednesday and Friday ● By Joe Bindloss*

Top Travel
Lists

Stimulating Hot Drinks to Break your Coffee Addiction

Forget your favourite latte. Quaff some global culture with this array of mouth-watering hot drinks from around the world.

1 Masala chai, India

Fashion-forward Mumbaikars, frazzled Delhi commuters, roadside marigold sellers – they all cock their ears at the call from a *chai wallah* (tea seller). Masala chai was originally brewed as a tonic to boost spirit and mind, comprising cardamom, ginger and other spices steeped in hot milk. Black tea became part of the recipe when the British East India Company introduced it to India in the 19th century. Today blends vary by region: clove, green tea, rose.
Some of India's most thirst-quenching teas originate in Darjeeling; try a delicate brew at Nathmull's Tea Room.

2 Mate, Argentina

For Argentines, sharing *mate* with friends is a national obsession. Locals gulp down more *mate* than they do coffee – and they *love* their coffee. Dried *yerba mate* leaves are shaken into a gourd and topped with hot water. The bitter infusion is sipped through a metallic straw, or *bombilla*, which also sifts out the herbs. The gourd is passed from person to person as a gesture of friendship, so sip away if it's offered (and don't risk offence by fiddling with the *bombilla*). It's not only the social experience that will make you smile, *mate* is vitamin rich and teeming with antioxidant properties.
Curious to learn more? Posadas and Tigre both have museums dedicated to mate.

3 Sbiten, Russia

It takes a fortifying beverage indeed to melt the grip of a Russian winter. Luckily *sbiten* has been thawing Russian noses since the 12th century – and boasts healing powers to boot. Honey, berry jam and pounded spices (often clover and thyme) are boiled with water in a shining copper samovar to make *sbiten*. The drink's health-boosting qualities are renowned, promising everything from a sturdy immune system to mental agility. Coffee may have replaced *sbiten* in Siberian thermoses in recent decades, but this bracing tipple is making a comeback; Russians even sip a chilled version during the warmer months.
Note that some sbiten *recipes contain a splosh of vodka or wine.*

4 Mint tea, Morocco

Most visitors to Morocco see their first cup of mint tea poured from a dramatic height. A drop is seldom spilled, and the grand display helps to cool the tea before it reaches the cup. This intoxicating nectar is made by bringing tea leaves to a furious boil with fresh mint and generous amounts of sugar.

The glasses in which mint tea is served – often brightly coloured with metallic tracery – attract as much praise as the drink itself. And serving this thirst-quencher is a byword for hospitality, with many Moroccans considering it impolite to refuse a second cup.

You might be offered complimentary mint tea while haggling in the bazaars of Fez or Marrakesh. Remember, accepting carries no obligation to buy.

Top Travel Lists ● ● ● ● ● ● ● ● ● ● ● ● ● ● ●

MOROCCAN MINT TEA, SERVED IN THE TRADITIONAL WAY

5 Bubble tea, Taiwan

From humble teahouse beginnings to a global craze, bubble tea has enjoyed a wild ride over its 30 years of existence. It began as a blend of condensed milk and hot black tea with a dollop of tapioca pearls, the '*boba*' that gave it the 'bubble tea' name. Today you can find it in flavours from watermelon to chocolate, and in a rainbow-defying palette of neon colours. Bubble tea graces menus everywhere from London to Hong Kong. It's also billed as 'pearl milk tea', featuring irresistible guest ingredients like flavoured jellies and fruit, and served chilled.

Go back to the source at the earliest known bubble teahouses in Taiwan, Chun Shui Tang in Taichung or Hanlin teahouse in Tainan.

ARGENTIAN *MATE* IS A NATIONAL INSTITUTION AND AN EXERCISE IN SOCIAL BONDING

6 Api morado, Bolivia

Bright magenta, soupily thick and irresistibly sweet, *api morado* is a truly unique breakfast drink. This blend of purple corn, cinnamon, cloves, sugar and hot water is a prized way to perk up in the frosty Andean air. Today it is blended with lemon, pineapple or other fruits and served with another Bolivian breakfast favourite, flaky empanadas. *Api* has an ancient heritage, and has been warming bellies since the days of the Inca Empire. As modern scientists learn more about purple corn's anti-inflammatory properties and excellent health benefits, it seems the Inca were on to something.

Don't limit yourself to purple api, *steamy white corn drinks are also popular in Bolivia.*

7 Po cha, Tibet

No traveller wants to wince in the face of hospitality. But for many people, *po cha* is an acquired taste. Creating 'butter tea' is a labour of love: black tea is steeped for hours before being churned with butter from female yaks and stirred with salt. This staple drink of the Tibetan mountains is perfectly suited to the high altitude: hugely hydrating and fattening enough to fortify labourers against the chill. But its earthy pungency can shock the taste buds at first. Imbibing it is highly ritualised, with hosts expected to top up a cup after each sip.

Po cha not to your taste? To avoid a refill from your host, wait until the end of your visit and gulp the tea down in one.

8 Sahlep, Turkey

Sweet Turkish coffee turbo-charges many a visitor around the palaces and bazaars of Istanbul. But Turkey's preferred winter warmer is *sahlep*, hot sweet milk infused with orchid root powder. Orchid-based drinks have a long history, used as an aphrodisiac by the Romans (who took the suggestive shape of the root rather literally). But while notions of *sahlep*'s romantic effects have been all but abandoned, the creamily nourishing beverage – with the faintest of floral notes – is enjoyed across the Middle East, sometimes sprinkled with orange blossom water, coconut or raisins.

Ask a local where to find authentic sahlep *in Turkey, as cheap cornflour-thickened imitations abound.*

9 Tieguanyin, China

Drink tea in China and you're partaking in an ancient tradition that remains a cornerstone of social interaction. One floral oolong variety in particular, *tieguanyin* (iron goddess of mercy tea), has a myth of origin placing it at the heart of China's sacred tea culture. Stories say that a poor farmer prayed for the means to repair a temple to the goddess, and dreamt of treasure. Awaking, he discovered a single shoot which brought forth the finest tea in China, restoring the temple's fortunes and thereafter being named after the merciful goddess.

Fill your neighbour's cup before pouring Chinese tea for yourself. If someone pours for you, indicate thanks by rapping your finger on the table.

> **Bright magenta, soupily thick and irresistibly sweet, api morado is a truly unique breakfast drink**

10 Anijsmelk, Netherlands

When winter freezes lakes and canals across the Netherlands, the Dutch reach for their ice skates. And a spin on the ice is traditionally accompanied by a glass of *anijsmelk*. This sweetened milk drink is infused with aniseed, giving it a smoky herbal note. For the Dutch it's a nostalgic flavour and those who want a fuss-free *anijsmelk* fix buy aniseed -flavoured sugar cubes. But it's best on a frosty Amsterdam evening, fragrant steam curling under your nose and fresh *poffertjes* (mini pancakes) warming your hands as you watch skaters swirl across the canals.

The love of liquorice flavours doesn't end here, the Dutch consume more than four pounds per person annually, mostly in the form of salty drop sweets.

● *By Anita Isalska*

Top Travel Lists

Most Sheepish Encounters

From wild flocks to woolly socks to lamb chops: we shepherd ewe through a global celebration of the Chinese Year of the Sheep

1 Jade Chinese zodiac, New York City, USA

As part of the Metropolitan Museum of Art's permanent collection of Chinese Decorative Arts, this zodiac is usually on display in Gallery 222 and always on display online. The rat, ox, tiger, hare, dragon, snake, horse, sheep, monkey, rooster, dog, and pig still have a significant role in Chinese culture; in 2015 the Year of the Sheep (sometimes interchanged with a goat) starts on 19 February. Early zodiacs were depicted in wall paintings of the 6th century; pottery figurines were popular in the Tang dynasty (618–907); the Met's jade animals are 19th-century.

The Met is closed Thanksgiving Day (26 November 2015), 25 December, 1 January and the first Monday in May (4 May 2015). See www. metmuseum.org.

2 Giant ram, Wagin, Australia

It's a long way, geographically and culturally speaking, from the Big Apple of New York to the Big Sheep of Wagin, Western Australia. But 'big things' are a welcome diversion on the long unwinding roads of the Australian outback; one of several big sheep around the country, this giant ram stands an impressive 7m tall and 15m long and gazes across the town, a monument to the local merino industry that helped to fund Wagin's historic streetscape, established in 1889.

Three hours' drive south from Perth, time a visit to Wagin to coincide with the annual 'Woolorama', one of Western Australia's biggest agricultural shows, held in March.

3 Barbary sheep, North Africa

Hardy Barbary sheep are Africa's only wild sheep. Called *aoudad* by the region's Berber people, they're found in barren mountains where they somehow manage to find enough water from vegetation and dew to survive. Barbaries have an exceptional ability to remain motionless and barely visible when threatened – handy, given that their heavy horns lure hunters in countries where they have been introduced, such as the USA. Seeing them in the wild requires time, patience and good local knowledge: WWF-US runs tours to the Sahara and Atlas Mountains in Morocco, one of the sheep's native habitats.

Check out www.worldwildlife.org/tours and their partner Natural Habitat Adventures www.nathab.com.

4 Dolly the sheep, Edinburgh, Scotland

Dolly (5 July 1996–14 February 2003), a Finn Dorset sheep, made world headlines and graced the cover of *Time* magazine in 1997. She was the first mammal to be cloned from adult (sheep) cells, and the only one from 277 cloning attempts to survive to adulthood. Why was she called Dolly? Ian Wilmut, one of the cloners, said 'Dolly is derived from a mammary gland cell and we couldn't think of a more impressive pair of glands than Dolly Parton's'. Dolly's stuffed remains are on show in the Science and Technology galleries at the National Museum of Scotland.

The museum is open daily except for Christmas Day: admission is free. See www.nms.ac.uk.

MERINO SHEEP IN OTAGO, NEW ZEALAND

Top Travel ● ● ● ● ● ●
Lists ● ● ● ● ● ● ●

5 Museum of Norwegian Knitting Industry, Norway

Between 1859 and 1989, Salhus Tricotagefabrik made fine woollens; it was the first mechanised knitwear factory in Norway. Most of its products weren't seen in public though; the firm specialised in underwear. The factory reopened as a museum in 2001; guides unravel the mysteries of carding, spooling and knitting during daily tours and machines with cogs and wheels of polished brass are kept in working order. There are hands-on workshops for kids on alternate Sundays.
Salhus village is about 16km north of Bergen, Norway's second-largest city.

6 Sheep dog trials, Ontario, Canada

Although open to all breeds of dog, Border collies rule the roost in the annual sheep dog trials in Kingston, Ontario. Finalists compete in the Gather (fetching sheep), the Drive (taking sheep through an obstacle course), the Shed (separating five sheep from the flock) and the Pen (leading these five sheep to a separate pen). The co-stars are 600 Dorset ewes, with just a hint of exotic Romanov and rural Cheviot in their heritage. Sideshows are kid-heaven, including sheep shearing and pony rides.
2015 is the trials' 28th anniversary: see www.kingstonsheepdogtrials.com.

7 Sheep shearing, New Zealand

Get up close and personal with the woolly mainstay of New Zealand's economy: near Queenstown, several farms offer tours that include sheep feeding, petting and shearing. Sound too low-key? For a more competitive view of the industry, visit the Golden Shears championship in Masterton. Held annually since 1958, this three-day event in late February or early March hosts eye-popping sessions of speed-shearing, wool handling and wool pressing. And if it all gets too much, relax in the paddock with the four-legged participants.
See www.queenstownnz.co.nz and www.goldenshears.co.nz Some championship events, including the speed-shear and wool sculpting, are free for spectators and artists respectively.

> One Uighur speciality that makes use of the sheep from head to tail is morxueke; a whole sheep banquet

8 Sheepskin clothing, Nepal

In the swinging '60s, sheepskin coats were high fashion for hippies. Today they remain functional – rather than fashionable – winter wear for mountain people throughout Asia: sheepskin, unlike leather, is tanned with the fleece intact which means an extra layer of effective insulation. In villages in Nepal, traditional wear for Sherpa men is a long-sleeved robe called a *chhuba*, tied at the waist with a cloth sash called a *kara*. Chhuba were made from thick home-spun wool, and a variant called *lokpa* was made from sheepskin. Women traditionally wear long-sleeved floor-length dresses of thick wool called *tongkok*.
Ask around the Thamel market, in Nepal's capital Kathmandu, for sheepskins, woollen carpets and knitwear.

THE WHOLE SHEEP BANQUETS IN XINJIANG, CHINA ARE FLAVOURED WITH A SPICE MIX THAT INCLUDES CUMIN AND DRIED HOT RED PEPPERS

9 Whole sheep banquet, Xinjiang, China

Mutton reigns supreme in this mostly Muslim region. One Uighur speciality that makes use of the sheep from head to tail is *morxueke*; a whole sheep banquet where each body part contributes to several separate dishes including a sort of spicy intestinal haggis. Just as tasty but possibly less confronting (and certainly easier to access) is the food at Xibo Restaurant in Shanghai, where lamb is sourced locally and dishes lean heavily on traditional Uighur recipes.

For more about Xinjiang in general and Xibo's fair-trade food ethics in particular see www.xiboxinjiang.com.

10 The Woolsack, London, England

Seat of the Lord Speaker in the House of Lords, the Woolsack is a large square bale of wool, covered in red cloth, with no arms or back. The tradition dates back to the 14th-century reign of Edward III, when the wool trade was the country's most important industry and the Woolsack was stuffed only with precious English wool. More recently, in a scandalous revelation in 1938, it was discovered that the Woolsack was in fact filled with horsehair! These days it is stuffed with wool from around the Commonwealth.

To arrange a real visit or take a virtual tour of the House of Lords, see www.parliament.uk.
● *By Virginia Jealous*

Top Travel Lists

Top Places to Feel Like You're in the Future

As Back to the Future *turns 30, let these locales sweep you in for a peep at how the present might appear several decades from now...*

1 Tokyo, Japan

Tokyo has long been regarded as a bastion of state-of-the-art, from its fine dining (more Michelin stars than London and New York combined) to its toilets (automatically raising lids and heated seats). If you want to travel, trains capable of 200mph whisk you out of the capital. If you're thirsty, vending machines predict your drink choice before you select (via sensors, based on your appearance and the weather). But technology sometimes thwarts even the Japanese. Plans for the enormous Shimizu Pyramid, a housing solution proposal for one million of the space-cramped population that would sit spread-eagled over Tokyo Bay, have been postponed: construction materials strong enough don't currently exist.

Ultra-modern Jicoo Floating Bar (www.jicoofloatingbar.com) is a snazzy boat that cruises around Tokyo Bay, resembling the pleasure craft of a megalomaniac Bond villain.

2 McMurdo Station, Ross Island, Antarctica

It's a vision of what human colonisation on another planet might resemble. A scattered community of low-level buildings dwarfed by immense circular fuel storage tanks, which in turn are rendered miniscule by barren mountains that rear up behind the Antarctic's largest research facility in layers of snow-flecked volcanic ash. The inhabitants of this strange land? Dive-bombing skuas, penguins, and scientists devoted to discovering how our planet ticks – or, perhaps, is ticking away The station is as autonomous as another planet's colony would be, too: sporting restaurants, a gym, a hospital, a chapel, and with cross-country skiing equipment to borrow.

To discover more about McMurdo, watch Werner Herzog's Encounters at the End of the World, *a documentary focusing on residents' daily lives there.*

3 Dubai, United Arab Emirates

The time-travelling protagonists of *Back to the Future* would have oohed no end at Dubai's audacious portfolio of buildings that seem beamed from decades yet to be. Think soaring tapered towers, metallic dhows and an artificially created archipelago that fans out into the ocean in the shape of a palm: city architecture resonates with tomorrow's possibilities. But stay tuned. Dubai won the bid to host Expo 2020 – where exhibitors will be ensconced in a futuristic-looking souk with mammoth solar-powered sunshades. Expect innovation to keep on coming.

Climb to the summit of the world's tallest building, the Burj Khalifa (www.burjkhalifa.ae/en), to observe Dubai's bizarre cityscape.

Top Travel Lists ● ● ● ● ● ● ● ● ● ● ● ● ● ●

4 Ordos, Inner Mongolia, China

Its name sounds like something from *Star Wars*. The apartment blocks of the city's Kangbashi neighbourhood stand largely empty despite being designed to house thousands, and main roads are deserted even at 'rush hour'. Yet Ordos, China's best-known ghost town (the expected inhabitants just never came), has a stronger case for being deemed the world's most sci-fi-esque address. Just beyond the city limits, is the Ordos Museum – a sinuous shell plonked on the desert's edge and housing exhibitions about the region's culture.

The Kubuqi Desert is west of Ordos on route G109 then north on X613.

5 Toronto, Canada

Dubai of the north? Mini-New York? Toronto's nicknames are indicative of the real estate boom continuing to shape the city's skyline. Just being tall and glassy isn't enough to make an impact in a North American downtown any more: certainly not in the city with the western hemisphere's highest free-standing structure, the CN Tower. New construction projects must be at least a little outlandish to impress. Enter the Absolute Towers – twin condominiums of 50- and 56-storeys that twist 209 degrees from base to top – and the Emerald Park Condos, resembling chocolate bars with the wrapping partially peeled back. It's all building towards Toronto looking like a sci-fi comic.

Leading architects have contributed to Toronto's iconic buildings; learn about them on a walking tour with Heritage Toronto (heritagetoronto.org/programs/tours/walks).

THE ORDOS MUSEUM IN INNER MONGOLIA, CHINA LOOKS LIKE A LANDED CRAFT FROM OUTER SPACE

6 Hammarby Sjöstad, Stockholm, Sweden

Built as the athletes' village for Sweden's failed 2004 Olympics bid, this eco-town outside Stockholm has transformed into a model of low-key sustainability, with water heating half supplied by solar panels and recycling rooms in every building. Hammarby Sjöstad also focuses on aesthetics. It's a tranquil, lakefront community with canal-side walks, parks and not a flash of showy glass and steel in sight. *Back in central Stockholm, don't miss a ride on the subway, boldly painted by local artists*

7 New Songdo City, Incheon, South Korea

Take a smidgeon of the Sydney Opera House, a dose of Venice and a chunk of New York's Central Park. Mix well. The result, say the people behind Songdo, will be just what they are designing: a city of cutting-edge architecture, bisected by canals and green spaces. Completion is scheduled for 2020 but green spaces totalling 40% of Songdo's area, many apartment blocks, a convention centre of glitzy prisms and a pneumatic waste collection system negating the need for rubbish trucks already stand vanguard over Incheon's waterfront. *You can stay at Songdo's first hotel, Sheraton Incheon Hotel (www.sheratonincheon.com).*

8 Spaceport America, Las Cruces, New Mexico, USA

Public space travel is likely to be off the ground by the time you read this, though at US$250,000 a seat, it's not cheap. Visitors to Virgin Galactic's 62 sq km launch pad facility, in an already otherworldly desert landscape, can gawk at the monolithic domed space operations centre, and the vast fuel tanks required for stocking up for missions. *Official tour operator Follow the Sun (ftstours.com) embellishes its Spaceport tours with updates on the latest in space technology*

9 Abu Dhabi, United Arab Emirates

Abu Dhabi's under-construction Saadiyat Cultural District bristles with buildings that seem just-landed from a far more advanced civilisation. Plans feature a Guggenheim (a gigantic mound of cubes and open-ended cones) and Zayed International Museum (which whirls up in a flurry of steel wings representing the late Sheikh Zayed Bin Sultan Al Nahyan's penchant for falconry). Southeast of centre, the ambitious arcology project of Masdar City is intended to be car-free and powered 100% by renewable energy. *Read more about Abu Dhabi's awe-inspiring architecture at www.saadiyatculturaldistrict.ae.*

10 Singapore

Of all Asia's metropolises, Singapore is most glamorously futuristic. buildings like the Marina Bay Sands hotel/casino complex (three towers joined up top by a sky-park, pictured overleaf) have become distinctive landmarks. But the most ingenious development yet is more green than glassy. The tropical gardens at Gardens by the Bay feature 18 50m-high super-trees, connected via walkways to two giant, greenhouses that act as biomes for thousands of non-native plants. *Get a flavour of what the gardens offer at www. gardensbythebay.com.sg.* ● *By Luke Waterson*

Most Illuminating Experiences

2015 is the UN Year of Light – so make a beeline for these brilliantly bright, bedazzling places.

1 Aurora, Abisko, Sweden

The northern lights shimmer right across the polar regions – if solar activity is particularly exuberant you might even glimpse the lights as far south as Scotland. But, really, to maximise your chances of seeing aurora action, head for Abisko's Aurora Skystation, nearly 200km north of the Arctic Circle and a long way from pretty much anything else. The surrounding mountains keep the skies almost always clear; light pollution is zero; and long winter nights provide the perfect black canvas for the heavenly glow.

Abisko's Aurora Sky Station (www.auroraskystation.com) is 100km west of Kiruna. The best time to visit is September to March.

> **Long winter nights provide the perfect black canvas for the heavenly glow**

2 Marfa Lights, Texas, USA

As illuminating experiences go, this one really isn't – you can see the Marfa Lights flashing over the Chihuahuan Desert and still not have a clue what they are. About the size of basketballs, these odd reddish orbs flicker over Mitchell Flat, 16km east of Marfa; witnesses say they split, merge and morph in a most peculiar fashion. Science hasn't yet figured it out; head to the specially constructed viewing platform at Mitchell Flat and ponder for yourself.

Marfa is accessible via Highway 90. The nearest airport is El Paso, 305km west.

3 Lanterns, China

The Chinese have been celebrating the Lantern Festival for over 1000 years – though in many different forms. Over the centuries the end-of-winter event has included elements of Buddhist worship, riddle-solving, folk-dancing and even matchmaking (it was the one night of the year when girls were allowed out, perhaps to meet Mr Right). These days, it's mainly an incandescent occasion, when streets countrywide are paraded by innumerable lanterns in all shapes and sizes, from traditional round-red to dramatic dragons. Proceedings are particularly bright in Zigong, Sichuan province, where the festival has been celebrated since Tang times, and lantern-making has become a fine art.

The Lantern Festival falls on the 15th day of the first lunar month, usually February or March; 5 March in 2015.

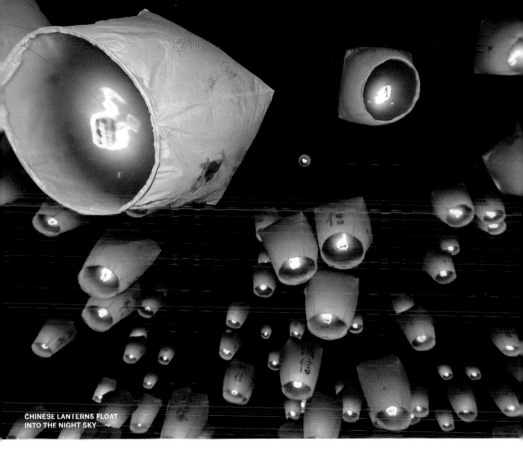

CHINESE LANTERNS FLOAT
INTO THE NIGHT SKY

4 Midnight sun, Svalbard, Norway

Wish there were more hours in the day? No problem: plan a summer trip to Svalbard. Nudging the North Pole, this Arctic archipelago has long, dark, gloomy winters but makes up for it come spring: in capital Longyearbyen the midnight sun lasts from 15 April to 26 August. That's more than four months of relentless rays, the sun never dipping below the horizon. Make the most of all this light: once the seas are accessible (usually from June), board an expedition cruise and spend the wee hours on deck watching calving glaciers, grunting walruses and polar bears patrolling the pack ice. Wild nights indeed.

There is no ferry service between Svalbard and Norway; Longyearbyen is served by flights from Oslo.

Top Travel ● ● ● ● ● ● ●
Lists ● ● ● ● ● ● ●

5 Stars, NamibRand Nature Reserve, Namibia

The vast NamibRand Nature Reserve is really, really dark. Which is why it's such a good place to see the light. Designated a gold-standard International Dark Sky Reserve in 2012, this 202,200-hectare patch of private wilderness is a fence-free sanctuary for wildlife, and a blank slate for the universe. There is simply no light pollution here, and thus nothing to diminish the majesty of the southern hemisphere's night sky. The reserve's Sossusvlei Desert Lodge even has a state-of-the-art observatory, complete with Meade LX200R 12-inch telescope, so you can take an even more intimate look at all that glitters above.
Sossusvlei Desert Lodge is 380km from Windhoek; the drive takes 4 to 5 hours; see www.namibrand.com.

6 Firefly squid, Toyama Bay, Japan

It's like the sea is having a really big party. Every year, from March to May, the waters of north-central Honshu's Toyama Bay start to sparkle like a glitterball. The revellers responsible are weeny *Watasenia scintillans* – firefly squid; they measure just 7cm long but come here in their millions to spawn in spring. Their bodies are covered in photophores, light-producing organs that flash and pulsate in patterns of brilliant blue. Perhaps they do it to communicate, to confuse predators, or to attract prey – but they certainly manage to amaze.
Boat trips to see the squid run March to May, at around 3am; enquire at Namerikawa's Hotaruika (firefly squid) Museum.

7 Fluorescence, Amsterdam, Netherlands

No need to indulge in the famed cafe narcotics to have your mind blown in Amsterdam – Electric Ladyland will do the job. It's the world's first (and surely only?) Museum of Fluorescent Art, where visitors descend into an underground dayglo gallery, full of surreal shapes and psychedelic bulges. In other rooms you can learn about the history of fluorescence and see large collections of rocks, which appear drab until they react radiantly to UV light.
The museum is at Tweede Leliedwarsstraat 5 (www. electric-lady-land.com).

Float through one of Waitomo's caverns and it's like being in a fairytale: the 300-million-year-old labyrinth seems to have a ceiling of stars

8 Neon lights, Las Vegas, USA

According to NASA, Las Vegas is the brightest place on the planet. No surprise there: the glowing gamblers' den has billions of bulbs, with an estimated 15,000 miles of neon tubing on the Strip alone. The result is a blazing hole in the Nevada Desert, from the tacky twinkles of Chapel O Love signs to the Luxor Hotel's Sky Beam – the strongest beam in the world. However, don't miss the Neon Museum Boneyard, where all those lights go to die.
The Neon Museum (770 Las Vegas Blvd) offers day and night tours (www.neonmuseum.org).

9 Glowworms, Waitomo, New Zealand

Descend into the Waitomo Caves on New Zealand's North Island to meet *Arachnocampa luminosa*. Lots of them. Glowworms thrive here and while these slimy bugs don't look so pretty when the lights are on, in the dark they sparkle like Christmas. Float through one of Waitomo's caverns, by boat or by inflatable tube, and it's like being in a fairytale: the 300-million-year-old labyrinth seems to have a ceiling of stars. That the gleam comes from a chemical reaction designed to lure in prey doesn't decrease the magic.

Waitomo Caves is 200km (around a three-hour drive) south of Auckland; see www.waitomo.com.

10 Festival of Lights, Berlin, Germany

Berlin never looks more brilliant than during its Festival of Lights. For 10 days each October, the landmarks and thoroughfares of the German capital become 3D canvases for a glittering array of art installations: they are projected onto buildings from 7pm until midnight, making the whole city a swirl of colour and creativity. 'Lightseeing' tours – by bus, boat, boot or segway – are available, but just eyeballing the illuminations is completely free.

The festival runs for 10 days in mid-October; a full program can be found at festival of lights.de
- *By Sarah Baxter*

BERLIN'S CATHEDRAL COMES ALIVE WITH COLOUR EVERY OCTOBER FOR THE FESTIVAL OF LIGHTS

Top Travel Lists

Wonderful Workouts

Exercise on holiday needs neither to be boring, nor a waste of valuable travel time. Hit these locations hard and you'll experience a rush of more than just endorphins.

1 Grouse Grind, North Vancouver, Canada

Visitors looking for a little exercise in Vancouver traditionally head to the stunning 8.8km Stanley Park Seawall. And who can blame them? But if you want a sharp hit of dramatic mountain fitness (and beauty), head to the North Shore and tackle the Grouse Grind. The Grind, which rises 853m up the forest-clad face of Grouse Mountain

IT'S A STEEP CLIMB UP GROUSE GRIND IN VANCOUVER, BUT CLIMBERS ARE REWARDED WITH PANORAMIC VIEWS FROM THE SUMMIT

in just 2.9km of trail (including 2830 stairs), is unsurprisingly referred to as 'Mother Nature's Stairmaster'. An average newcomer time is 90 minutes (the record is 25 minutes). If you're broken, ride the gondola back. If not, enjoy the exhaustion on the faces of those you pass on the trot down.

The Grind is free, but if you'd like to set an official time (and have your bag ferried up) buy a Grind Timer Card for C$20 at www.grousemountain.com.

2 Fourvière, Lyon, France

For decades Lyon has been called the food capital of the world, and for good reason. A trip here is simply not complete without a serious (and perhaps gluttonous) gastronomic exploration. So how better to tackle your excesses (or build up your appetite for more) than by running up the hundreds of steps from Gare St Paul to Basilica Notre Dame de Fourvière? The grandiose basilica is a reward in itself, as is the panoramic view over the rivers Rhône and Saône meandering beautifully through the city. Want more? Reverse step one and repeat, or hit the many steps that climb Lyon's La Croix-Rousse hill.

The Basilica Notre Dame de Fourvière is open 8am to 7pm. For information about guided tours visit www.fourviere.org.

3 Filbert Steps, San Francisco, USA

San Francisco's Telegraph Hill is known for different things to different people. To some it's the home of the iconic Coit Tower. To others it's simply a good place to get a fantastic view over San Francisco Bay. To those who enjoy serious leg-, lung- and buttock-burning exercise, the hill is the site of the Filbert Steps. For a workout you won't soon forget, run up and down the 377 narrow wooden steps, which meander steeply through verdant vegetation and past colourfully clad homes. You may even be serenaded by a wild parrot or two. Don't leave your heart in San Francisco – strengthen it there.

The base of the Filbert Steps is found at the junction of Filbert and Kearny Streets.

4 Circuit de Monaco, Monaco

Perhaps the most famous section of city streets in the world, the 2.075-mile Circuit de Monaco has seen race cars scream around its corners and through Monte Carlo's famed Casino Square since 1929. While modern Formula One drivers will see little but a blur of the plush principality when taking the circuit on, you can soak it all as you run around it (how many laps is up to you). Much like those strapped into an F1 car, your heart will race; the climb up Avenue d'Ostende after rounding Sainte Devote is a steep one. Finish with a plunge in the Mediterranean at Plage du Larvotto.

You'll find the F1 starting grid painted onto Boulevard Albert 1er above the harbour's swimming pool complex. GO! GO! GO!

The steps meander steeply through verdant vegetation and past colourfully clad homes. You may even be serenaded by a wild parrot or two

Top Travel ● ● ● ● ● ● ● ●
Lists ● ● ● ● ● ● ● ●

5 Table Mountain, Cape Town, South Africa

Thanks to a scenic aerial cableway, a trip to the top of Table Mountain is simply a fun day out for most visitors to Cape Town. But you're not like most people. Your journey to the top will be a workout you'll continue savouring long after your muscles stop aching. The Patteklip Gorge, which cuts the mountain's main face in two, is your most direct route up. The steep trail climbs almost 700m in a mere 3km. *The Patteklip Gorge route starts on Tafelberg Rd. Visit www.sanparks. org for trail safety advice and park information.*

6 Arthur's Seat, Edinburgh, Scotland

Edinburgh is one of Europe's most beautiful cities, and it's home to one of the continent's most rewarding workouts too. Head into Holyrood Park for an 8km run through its verdant volcanic playground. With sublime views of Edinburgh Castle, the Scottish Parliament and the sea, you'll feel like you're embracing the city. At other points, when you're hemmed in by rocky crags and swaying grasses, you'll feel away from it all. The high point, literally, is the summit of Arthur's Seat at the halfway mark. *Start from the car park on Queen's Drive, a 250m walk from Holyrood Palace at the end of the Royal Mile.*

FEEL THE BURN CLIMBING SAN FRANCISCO'S FILBERT STEPS

7 Central Park, New York City, USA

Arguably the most iconic of the world's urban running routes is the 2.5km loop around the Jacqueline Kennedy Onassis Reservoir in New York City's Central Park. The cinder pathway is soft under foot, so your knees won't hate you for pushing that extra bit harder (and longer), though the views of the city's skyline may rob you of breath. A great time to wrap up your workout is at dusk, when the setting sun reflects off the urban landscape. Watch the city's lights start to sparkle as the night creeps in.

Run around the reservoir anti-clockwise, and on the right side of the path. For more information visit www.centralpark.com.

8 Copacabana Beach, Rio De Janeiro, Brazil

Working your body out and showing it off collide in spectacular fashion on Copacabana. Absorb the unique vibe with a run or rollerblade along the beach's wide 4km-long promenade. Bump this up to 8km (16km return) if you include Ipanema Beach to the south. If you'd rather throw some weights around, there are several outdoor exercise stations and chin-up bars along Copacabana. Feeling bold? The final fitness frontier is to test your mettle against Cariocas in beach volleyball or football. How

much showing off you do in the process, whether of sporting prowess or of your toned physique, is up to you.

Workouts are best in the early morning before temperatures rise. Although the beach is lit at night, it's not wise to hang around after dark.

> **A great time to wrap up your workout is at dusk, when the setting sun reflects off the urban landscape**

9 Berlin Wall Trail, Berlin, Germany

To quote Freddie Mercury: 'Get on your bikes and ride!' Enhance your brawn and enrich your brain while cycling around the 160km Berlin Wall Trail, a well-signposted route dotted with interesting historical information about the infamous wall. Learn about the division of Germany, the building and falling of the wall, and of the tragedies of those who lost their lives trying to escape it. The trail is broken up into 14 sections, which range from 7 to 21km in length, so you can take on as little or as much of it as you'd like.

The beginning and end of each section is reachable by public transport (most services allow bicycles on board). For more information visit www.berlin.de/mauer/mauerweg/index/index.en.php.

10 Coast To Coast walkway, Auckland, New Zealand

They say walkway. We say runway. Challenge yourself with this 16km route through the city of Auckland, taking you from the Pacific Ocean to the Tasman Sea. Along the way you'll pass some of the city's architectural gems, and no fewer than five volcanic sites, some of which have been shaped and terraced by the Maori over the past 600 years. The route starts in Viaduct Harbour and ends in Manukau. It's part of the 3000km-long Te Araroa (The Long Pathway), which runs the length of the country.

Maps and information regarding the Coast to Coast are available at www.aucklandcouncil.govt.nz.

● *By Matt Phillips*

Best Literary Walking Tours

There's no better way to pay tribute to your favourite author or characters than to follow in their footsteps via these entertaining tours.

1 Millennium Tour, Stockholm, Sweden

The march of grim Scandinavian crime thrillers was spearheaded by Stieg Larsson's novel *The Girl with the Dragon Tattoo*, and this walk in the picturesque Swedish capital lets you relive the drama. Taking in the hip suburb of Södermalm, home to ace journalist Mikael Blomkvist and rogue IT genius Lisbeth Salander, the walk passes fictional sites mentioned in the Millennium trilogy, including Blomkvist's home, his local cafe, Salander's favourite tattoo parlour, Inspector Bublanski's synagogue, *Millennium* magazine's offices and, finally, Salander's luxury apartment. It's an atmospheric walk which helps colour in the dark outlines of Scandi noir.
Takes place in English 11.30am each Saturday, tickets 130 Swedish krona. Book via www.stadsmuseet. stockholm.se.

2 Literary Pub Crawl, Dublin, Ireland

This combination of tour and live performance highlights the rich cultural heritage of the Irish capital. Weaving between pubs that once hosted great writers such as James Joyce, Brendan Behan, Samuel Beckett and WB Yeats, tour members are entertained by readings, music and song. The tour passes literary sites such as Trinity College, where Oscar Wilde once studied. But the focus is firmly on the drinking holes where so much creativity flowed, from those featured in Joyce's epic novel *Ulysses* to Behan's old local. Raise a glass to their memory on the way.
Departs nightly in summer, cost €12. Book via www.dublinpubcrawl.com.

3 Literary Landmarks, Boston, USA

In the 19th century Boston was a hotbed of literature, spawning influential movements such as American Romanticism, American Realism and Transcendentalism. The Fireside Poets, including Henry Wadsworth Longfellow, triumphed here with their popular verse; joining other literary stars such as Ralph Waldo Emerson, Henry David Thoreau, Louisa May Alcott, Henry James and Nathaniel Hawthorne. This tour reveals their haunts, including the secret of the Saturday Club. *The tour proceeds in any weather. Fee US$12, book at www.bostonbyfoot.org.*

4 James Bond's Mayfair, London, UK

'Shaken, not stirred.' James Bond creator Ian Fleming coined this classic line while sipping cocktails at his favourite bar in London's exclusive Mayfair district. This and other classified secrets are revealed on this tour conducted by guide Simon Rodway, who's thoroughly researched Fleming's life and its connections to his famous fictional creation. From the author's birthplace through Berkeley Square to St James, tour members pass places with links to 007, including a naval club which evokes the author's wartime experience in military intelligence. You can order the cocktail created by Bond, the Vesper, at the end. *Available by commission, see www. silvercanetours.com. For posh lodgings with a modern twist in the area, stay at the Athenaeum (athenaeumhotel.com).*

THE WORLD HERITAGE TOWN OF BATH WAS ONCE HOME TO JANE AUSTEN

Top Travel Lists ●●●●●●●● ●●○●●●●●

5 Greenwich Village Literary Pub Crawl, New York City, USA

This tour through the Big Apple's famous Greenwich Village drops into several pubs that were once the site of writers' inspiration. Guides relate the stories of both the bars and the creative types who drank there, paying tribute to such famous local luminaries as Thomas Paine (author of *Common Sense*), John Reed (*Ten Days that Shook the World*), Henry James (*Washington Square*) and Edith Wharton (*Age of Innocence*); as well as less-remembered authors such as Dawn Powell (*Wicked Pavilion*) and Djuna Barnes (*Nightwood*). *Departs every Saturday at 2pm, fee US$20. Book tickets and browse a reading list at www. literarypubcrawl.com.*

> **Père Lachaise Cemetery has memorials to greats such as Molière, Proust and Wilde**

6 Writers in Paris, France

In the early 20th century the French capital was a magnet for writers, as detailed by American writer and Paris resident David Burke in this series of walks. There are four main tours, including 'A Band of Outsiders', which focuses on the Latin Quarter and the exploits of James Joyce, Ernest Hemingway and George Orwell, as well as celebrated French writers such as Honoré de Balzac and Victor Hugo. Other walks focus on the 'Lost Generation' of Montparnasse, the literary cafes of Saint-Germain-des-Prés, and Père Lachaise Cemetery's memorials to greats such as Molière, Proust and Wilde. *Check out writersinpariswalkingtours.blogspot. co.uk for these and additional special tours.*

7 Literary Shanghai, China

Shanghai's literary heyday came during the 19th and early 20th centuries, a period when colonial traders rubbed shoulders with the local population. Starting with a talk from knowledgeable guides at a local teahouse, this tour takes place in Hongkou in the city's north. It's an area associated with great local writers, including Lu Xun, the father of modern Chinese literature. The walk also visits a backstreet neighbourhood where the romantic poet Xu Zhimo once lived and hosted guests such as Indian writer Rabindranath Tagore and Irish writer George Bernard Shaw. *This tour is occasionally scheduled but otherwise operates by commission; for fees and bookings email publicwalks@shanghai-flaneur.com.*

8 Jane Austen in Bath, UK

It is a fact universally acknowledged that a Jane Austen fan visiting England must be in want of a good walking tour. Well, good sir or madam, here it is, and in a delightful city as a bonus. Bath is renowned for its graceful architecture. It was also where the famed author lived, and became the setting for her novels *Northanger Abbey* and *Persuasion*. The Jane Austen Centre leads this walking tour of literary highlights each weekend. *Tours depart 11am on Saturdays, Sundays and public holidays, fee £12. Book and find out more about Austen's Bath at www.janeausten.co.uk.*

VISIT THE PÈRE LACHAISE CEMETERY IN PARIS TO FIND MEMORIALS TO SOME OF THE GREAT WRITERS OF THE 20TH CENTURY

9 Melbourne Literary Tour, Australia

This Australian city is at the heart of the nation's literary scene, having become a UNESCO City of Literature in 2008. Delving into a tradition of writers, bookshops and publishers stretching from the colonial era, this tour offered by Melbourne Walks explores literary highlights in the city centre. Along the way, tour members dip into both the present and the past: visiting the Nicholas Building, for example, a so-called 'vertical laneway' of writers, bookshops and publishers; and imagining the past glory of Cole's Book Arcade, a well-remembered Victorian-era bookshop which once spanned a city block.
By arrangement, contact melbwalks@gmail.com.

10 Wild Walk Along the Enchanted Way, Romania

After the Berlin Wall fell in 1989, British writer William Blacker ventured into eastern Europe and ended up living for eight years in rural Romania. The resulting book, *Along the Enchanted Way*, recorded villages untouched by modernity, where daily life retained the rhythms of the Middle Ages. Wild Frontiers offers a 10-day tour of northern Romania following in Blacker's footsteps, including walks through the attractive Iza Valley and Rodna Mountains National Park.
The tour costs £1,575 exclusive of airfares (www. wildfrontierstravel.com). • *By Tim Richards*

Top Travel Lists

Best Places for Extreme Eating

Here's where to wrangle the world's weirdest foodstuffs into your stomach.

1 Rocky Mountain oysters, Montana, USA

Seafood in Montana? Uh, not exactly. Also known as prairie oysters, calf fries, cowboy caviar, and swinging beef, Rocky Mountain oysters are actually the deep-fried testicles of young bulls. Eating them is a tradition among western ranchers, who find themselves with a surplus of bovine cojones after the spring castrating season. While it may take balls (sorry, sorry) to bite into your first oyster, once you get a mouthful of the crispy-on-the-outside, creamy-on-the-inside goodness, you'll be back for seconds (luckily they come in pairs). See if you've got the, uh, stomach for them at the annual booze-soaked Testicle Festival in Clinton, Montana.

Get more info about the Testicle Festival at testyfesty.com.

2 Chapulines, Oaxaca, Mexico

Scientists say insects will likely be a major source of cheap protein in the future. Well, in the southern Mexican state of Oaxaca, they're way ahead of the curve. Here, grasshoppers known as chapulines have been a common bar snack and taco filling for ages. They're usually toasted with salt and chilli, which gives them a pleasant crunchiness and tang. In fact, if you didn't spot the tiny legs and antennae, you might easily think these crispy little critters were popcorn. But don't take our word for it – look for the baskets of chapulines at the Mercado Juarez in Oaxaca City.

Oaxaca City's Mercado Juarez is located between Flores Magón and Calle 20 de Noviembre.

3 Balut, Philippines

This Filipino delicacy of fertilised egg is better tasted than seen. Because peering at a tiny pink duck embryo, complete with half-formed beak and wing buds, might just put you off your snack. And that would be unfortunate, because balut is mighty delicious. Imagine scrambled egg mixed with tender chunks of poultry and just a smidge of pleasantly gamey liver. It's usually served as a street food, boiled in the shell and served with salt, spices and vinegar. Crack the top of the shell and sip out the liquid broth before tackling the meat and yolk.

Look for balut in the street markets of Manila, where it's sold by vendors with portable carts.

4 Snake soup, Hong Kong, China

A traditional treat in the rapidly vanishing working-class neighbourhoods of Hong Kong, this Cantonese delicacy tastes like ordinary hot and sour soup, complete with chunks of tofu and slivers of mushroom. But those strips of meat? They're not chicken. Considered warming for the blood, snake soup is only served in winter, and only in a handful of old-fashioned restaurants that keep live snakes in wooden boxes in the dining room. She Wong Lam, in Hong Kong's increasingly trendy Sheung Wan neighbourhood, is one of the few holdouts. Here, you can wash down your soup with a shot of snake-infused liquor. Bottoms up!

She Wong Lam is at 13 Hillier St in the Sheung Wan neighbourhood of Hong Kong Island.

5 Casu marzu, Sardinia, Italy

For most of us, the sight of food teeming with insects is an excellent indication that it should be thrown in the bin ASAP. But on the Italian island of Sardinia, the more maggots, the merrier when it comes to the local cheese known as *casu marzu*, which uses the larvae of the cheese fly for maximum fermentation. This gives the cheese a pungency unrivalled by the sharpest Cheddar or most biting blue.

The legal status of casu marzu is currently dubious due to EU health regulations. Try asking around a Sardinian cheesemonger's.

SNAKE SOUP IS A TRADITIONAL DELICACY IN HONG KONG

6 Virgin boy eggs, Dongyang, China

Funky eggs are a bit of a theme in Chinese cuisine. There are 'century eggs' preserved in ash and quicklime, eggs boiled in tea, and duck eggs packed in salty charcoal. But the funkiest of all is the so-called 'virgin boy egg' of Dongyang, a city of 800,000 in the eastern Zhejiang province. These eggs are soaked and then boiled in the urine of prepubescent boys, ideally under 10 years old, then served in all their ammonia-scented glory. Locals say the eggs have amazing health properties, such as preventing heat stroke and promoting good circulation. Sounds like urine for a treat!

Dongyang is about five hours by train from Shanghai.

7 Lutefisk, Minnesota, USA

Norwegian immigrants brought this aged fish dish to the Midwestern United States, where it's become far more common than it ever was in the motherland. As pale as a Norwegian in a Minnesota winter, lutefisk is white fish soaked in lye until it becomes nearly translucent. Its pungent odour belies a rather bland taste. It's the disturbingly gelatinous texture that presents the real challenge to eaters. The classic venue for lutefisk-tasting is at a lutefisk supper at one of Minnesota's many Lutheran churches or Sons of Norway lodges.

The Lutfisk Lover's Lifeline (www. lutfiskloverslifeline.com) keeps an up-to-date list of lutefisk suppers across the upper Midwest.

8 Witchetty grubs, Australia

A grub as big as your hand that leaks yellow goo and tastes like scrambled eggs? OK, colour us curious (and more than a little queasy). Aboriginal Australians have been chowing on these juicy insects since time immemorial, as they're an excellent source of protein. The grubs live underground, where they feed off the roots of

decaying trees. Women and children were traditionally responsible for digging up the fat, wriggling treats, typically eaten raw. As you're unlikely to find witchetty grubs on the menu of Sydney gastropubs or Melbourne bistros, sample them on a 'bush tucker' tour of the Outback.

Boshack Outback, a farm 90 minutes from Perth, offers Outback tours which include a taste of witchetty grubs (boshackoutback.com/australian-bush-tucker).

THE DURIAN IS UNDOUBTEDLY AN ACQUIRED – OR NOT-SO-ACQUIRED – TASTE...

Top Travel Lists ●●●●●●● ●●●●●●

9 *Guinea pig, Peru*

Many of us fondly remember our pet guinea pigs. So sweet! So fuzzy! So fond of nibbling on their food pellets and snoozing in their cedar shavings! Well, in the Andes Mountains of South America, the homeland of the guinea pig, the adorable rodents are what's for dinner. Known as 'cuy' in Peru, guinea pigs are eaten roasted, grilled and fried. Diners order either the front end or the back end of the cuy, much as one might order the breast or thigh quarter of a chicken. This is appropriate, as the cuy meat tastes very much like poultry. What's more, eating cuy is much better for the environment than eating beef, as raising guinea pigs causes a fraction of the carbon output of raising cows. *In the Peruvian city of Cusco, the restaurant Kusikuy (Calle Suecia 339) means 'happy little guinea pig' in Quechua. Maybe not so happy?*

10 *Durian, Singapore*

Incongruously un-food-like words such as 'turpentine', 'gym socks', 'toilet' and 'rotting corpse' pop up with disturbing frequency when food writers try to describe this wildly popular Southeast Asian 'king of fruits'. The size of a bowling ball with evil-looking jagged green spikes, the durian looks like nothing so much as a medieval weapon. But its true power lies in its smell, which is so strong it's banned on public transport in Singapore. Crack open the durian and scoop out its creamy yellow flesh, and you'll be rewarded with a sweet yet strange flavour halfway between vanilla pudding and onions. This is the definition of 'acquired taste'.

Many Singapore locals consider Kong Lee Hup Kee Trading on Pasir Ris to be the top durian stall in the country. ● *By Emily Matchar*

The Most Gay-friendly Places on the Planet

As more and more nations grant equality to same-sex couples, here's a list of the most progressive, inclusive and accepting destinations that open their arms to the LGBTQ traveller.

1 Copenhagen, Denmark

Denmark may be the home of Lego and at the forefront of New Nordic Cuisine, but importantly it made history in 1998 by becoming the first nation in the world to recognise registered same-sex partnerships. And at Denmark's heart is the relaxed beauty of its compact cobblestoned capital, Copenhagen (pictured). Copenhagen

is home to Europe's oldest openly gay bar, *Centralhjornet,* whose origins date back to the 1950s; as well as the hip and super-cool district of Vesterbro, which also happens to be the city's red-light district. One of the most tolerant and open communities in Europe, Copenhagen's functional yet edgy fashion scene, brilliant array of cocktail bars, excellent range of gay-friendly boutique accommodation and packed calendar of queer events make it the gay-friendliest place on Earth.

At 105.6m, City Hall Tower is one of the tallest buildings in Copenhagen and provides some of the best views of the cobblestoned city. In 2014, the adjoining square was named the 'Rainbow Square' in recognition of the quest for equal rights.

2 New Zealand

The Land of the Long White Cloud has long been lauded for its inclusive and progressive behaviour toward the LGBTQ community. In 1998 New Zealand was the first nation to adopt the label of 'Gay/Lesbian Friendly' when referring to businesses and accommodation – an initiative now recognised globally. The country offers a brilliant network of gay- and lesbian-friendly homestays which run the length and breadth of the country from the top of the semi-tropical North Island to the depths of the glacial South. Since passing same-sex marriage laws in 2013, New Zealand has actively promoted same-sex marriage tourism to the likes of Australia and other Pacific nations where equality laws are less progressive.

Gay Ski Week, part of Winter Pride, has become a perennial favourite on the queer calendar and takes place in picturesque Queenstown in late July or early August (see www.gayskiweekqt.com).

3 Toronto, Canada

Toronto continues to be a beacon for the LGBTQ traveller in North America, and Canada is hands down the most advanced and progressive nation in the Americas for the queer community. Toronto's The Village, located in Church-Wellesley, is the cultural queer hub of the city, bursting with galleries, theatres and gay-friendly businesses. Home to events such as Pride Week Celebrations, Pride March and Dyke March, gay sub-culture has blossomed and thrived in The Village for decades and it will soon be home to the world's first gay-focused athletic centre at 519 Church St.

Forget dressing as skeleton or witch, if you're attending the Village's fabulous Halloween Block Party, think Gwyneth Paltrow's pink Oscar gown or Lady Gaga's crab-hat (see www.churchwellesleyvillage.ca).

4 Palm Springs, USA

Located approximately 100 miles southeast of Los Angeles, Palm Springs is a sun-seekers' paradise where the sun shines almost all year round and where the city has embraced everything queer. Palm Springs provides the LGBTQ traveller with an amazing array of outdoor activities, excellent shopping and dining, and the world's best poolside lounging. Palm Springs also offers the largest volume of male- and female-only accommodation anywhere in the world (many of these places are clothing optional). Pack the SPF and make the most of the sun, boys and girls!

For the boys – one of the longest running clothing-optional gay resorts in Palm Springs is the '50s-style Escape Resort (www. escapepalmsprings.com), and for the girls – check out the Spanish-colonial-inspired Casita Laquita (www.casitaslaquita.com).

5 Sitges, Spain

The coastal city of Sitges rests approximately 35km southwest of Barcelona and is home to Spain's first ever gay disco, which opened back in the 1980s. It's now one of Europe's 'Big Four' destinations for the queer traveller. Its stretch of sandy, often clothing-optional beaches make it a favourite for the boys, but its eclectic calendar of events ensures that there's something for the entire community.

Europe's 'Big Four' also include Mykonos, Gran Canaria and Ibiza, all key stops on many same-sex-exclusive Mediterranean cruises. Check out cruises on www.gaywelcome.com.

6 Berlin, Germany

Every fetish you could ever dream up can be catered for in Berlin. Germany's wild side is on display here and Berlin proudly boasts a vibrant and inclusive gay history that dates back to the golden age of the 1920s. The districts of Schoneberg (which hosts Gay Pride), Kreuzberg and Prenzlauerberg provide a diverse range of clubs, bars and restaurants for sampling. With no 'closing time' in Berlin, the party never ends!

For the more adventurous, get your fetish on at Easter Fetish Week, or don some leather at Folsom Europe (folsomeurope.info).

7 Skiathos & Mykonos, Greece

Ever since Jackie Onassis started visiting the Greek island of Mykonos in the 1970s, gay men have been flocking to the island of whitewashed houses and flower-filled courtyards, seeking out glamour and the famous Mediterranean sun. For a less hedonistic holiday, the sandy beaches, crystal clear waters and pine forested hills of Skiathos offer a relaxed and authentic experience for the LGBTQ traveller.

The Elysium Hotel, an exclusively gay boutique hotel, is the perfect playground for hedonists heading to Mykonos town (www.elysiumhotel.com).

Berlin proudly boasts a vibrant and inclusive gay history that dates back to the golden age of the 1920s

8 New York City, USA

The Stonewall riots that occurred in the late '60s in Greenwich Village are synonymous with the birth of the modern gay-rights movement. The incredibly inclusive communities of the West Village, Chelsea and Hell's Kitchen provide a fabulous array of gay-friendly accommodation options. Littered with significant LGBTQ landmarks such as Christopher St, the Harvey Milk School, the Lesbian Herstory Archives and, hello, Broadway and the Theatre District, New York is a queer traveller's mecca. *If you're considering getting hitched while in the Big Apple, go to: www.cityclerk.nyc.gov/html/marriage/same_sex_couples.shtml.*

9 Reykjavik, Iceland

The world's northernmost capital, Reykjavik has been described as one of the friendliest places and most inclusive on Earth. In 2015, Reykjavik will host its 17th Gay Pride march (one of Europe's oldest queer parades), and the 11th Bears on Ice event. Iceland also has some of the world's most progressive laws. In 2006, same-sex couples were granted equal rights with their heterosexual counterparts without limitation. Wander behind waterfalls, descend into dormant volcanoes, or while away a day in one of the many geothermal lagoons – this is an adventurer's paradise.

To attend the Bears on Ice event, you'll need to register – www.bearsonice.org.

10 Montevideo, Uruguay

This is a controversial inclusion on the list given the conservativeness of many Central and South American nations. But Uruguay, the smallest of the South American nations, is the most progressive. In 2013, Uruguay was the first Latin American country to legalise same-sex marriage, and homosexuality has been decriminalised since 1934. The relaxed attitude present in the Uruguayan capital of Montevideo provides a brilliant juxtaposition to the hustle and bustle of the likes of Buenos Aires.

Although progressive in protecting the rights of the LGBTQ community, excessive PDA (public displays of affection) are not advised. ● By Chris Zeiher

A FESTIVAL-GOER WEARS THEIR COLOURS WITH PRIDE IN REYKJAVIK, ICELAND

Best Places to Bait a Hook

Whether it's pinning down piranha, battling black marlin or shrimping on horseback, fishing offers holiday fun and local insight. Not to mention dinner.

1 Salmon, Umba River, Kola Peninsula, Russia

Aurora borealis, reindeer herds, snow: Russia's Kola Peninsula is a winter wonderland beyond compare. But come spring, this Arctic eden morphs into a different kind of paradise: salmon heaven. Each May, fisherfolk flock to the Kola's 123km-long Umba River to cast for some of the finest, fattest Atlantic salmon on earth. The Umba is believed to have up to five salmon runs per year, making for an almost endless flow of fish. But nothing comes easy here: the Umba is isolated, the wading tough going, and anglers have to share their space with the greatest fish fans of them all: bears.

The Umba salmon season is May to the end of October, catch-and-release only. Head to www.murman.ru/guide/tourism/fishing-eng.shtml for info on fishing tours.

2 Giant black marlin, Cairns, Australia

On Australia's Great Barrier Reef, anyone with a snorkelling mask can find Nemo. But it takes a tough cookie to land a legend. The giant black marlin is one of the most coveted catches on the planet: weighing up to 750kg and able to swim up to 130km per hour, it has the ability to turn hardened game fishers (and, after several hours in battle, their wrists) to jelly. The stunning 250km stretch between Cairns and Lizard Island is the best place on earth to hook one: more giant black marlin are caught in these waters than in the rest of the world combined.

Marlin season in Cairns runs from early September to late December. Check out the Cairns Bluewater Game Fishing Club website for information: cairnsbluewatergfc.com.au.

3 Catfish, southern USA

Y'all hungry? Git noodlin'! Also known as cat-daddling, gurgling and hillbilly handfishing, noodling is the not-exactly refined art of shoving your hand into an underwater hole, waiting until you get bitten by a flathead catfish and wrestling the thrashing 'mudcat' to the surface. Noodling has its drawbacks (catfish have a lot of teeth, and you never know *what* is lurking in that hole) but the sport isn't just for masochistic kicks: Native Americans were highly skilled handfishers, and in many southern states, the practice has become a much-valued tradition passed down over generations. Solo noodling is a no-no; an online search will bring up plenty of expeditions for the wannabe cat-daddler. *Noodling is legal in Alabama, Arkansas, Georgia, Illinois, Kansas, Kentucky, Mississippi, North Carolina, Oklahoma, South Carolina, Tennessee, Texas and Wisconsin. Noodling season runs from May to August.*

4 Taimen, Eg-Uur River Basin, Mongolia

Think 'Mongolia', and it's yaks, nomads and exceptionally salty tea that probably spring to mind. But this remote central Asian outpost – more famous for steppes than streams – is one of the last remaining havens for the world's largest trout species, the taimen. A fierce, cannibalistic monster (they're known locally as 'river wolves'), taimen can grow up to 2m and smash the scales at 90kg; fishing for these whoppers is not for the faint of heart or the feeble of arm. The fish can live for up to 50 years, giving determined taimen trollers a lifetime to land the perfect beast. *Catch-and-release of taimen is strictly enforced. Mongolia's fishing season is June to November.*

A VIETNAMESE WOMAN SELLS FRESH AND DRIED SEAFOOD FROM HER BOAT IN HALONG BAY

5 Piranha, Amazon Basin, Brazil

It can happen to anyone: a few enjoyable hours watching piranha B-movies, and then bam! Aquaphobia! Since swimming is now off, why not spend your spare time fishing for the demons that turned you into a neurotic mess? Head to Manaus, capital of the Brazilian state of Amazonia, and join one of the many tours (pictured overleaf) that offer piranha fishing (and in some cases, eating). A hunk of meat lands them by the dozen but their razor teeth can cut through steel hooks as well as fingers. Exercise caution: in this fishing story, the only one that gets away should be *you*.

July to October is the dry season in the Amazon, and a dangerous time for piranha fishing, as the fish are hungry and aggressive. Tours can be organised through the Ariau Amazon Towers hotel in Manaus (www.ariautowers.com).

6 Shrimp, Oostduinkerke, Belgium

If you find rubbernecking an irresistible pastime, head to Oostduinkerke, on Belgium's southwest coast, where prawn fishermen – *paardenvissers* in Flemish – use not shrimpers but sturdy stallions to harvest the North Sea's fruits de mer. For the last 500 years, the fishermen have galloped into the sea on horseback, their steeds dragging nets and a wooden carriage (to scare the shrimp to the surface) through cold, crashing waves in a tradition recently recognised by UNESCO as being of 'intangible cultural heritage'. This four-legged fishing is best left to the experts, but lucky visitors can score a ride in the shrimp-scaring rig.

Oostduinkerke's horse-shrimping seasons are February–May and September–November. Contact Oostduinkerke's visitor centre at visitor.koksijde.be for more information.

7 Goliath tigerfish, Congo River Basin

For an adrenaline rush that really will send you reeling, head to the Congo to hunt down the goliath tigerfish, a terrifyingly toothy brute with a temper just as sharp. Africa's equivalent of the piranha, this aggressive predator has a history of attacking humans, and has been known to maul birds in flight. Growing up to 1.5m and weighing in at 70kg-plus, the mbenga (as it's known locally) is no easy catch: dangerous day-long battles have made it one of the world's greatest sports fishing challenges.

If you want to battle the mbenga, you must join an organised excursion for your own safety. The best time to catch one is during the Congo's dry season, June to October.

8 Ice fishing, Brainerd, USA

Do you like to dig holes in ice and stare into them for a long time? Then the central-Minnesota town of Brainerd is your dream destination. The annual Brainerd Jaycees Ice Fishing Extravaganza is the largest of its kind in the world, attracting more than 12,000 hopefuls keen on the cold... and on hooking themselves a cool US$150,000 worth of prizes. Organisers pre-drill 20,000 holes into the thankfully very well-frozen Gull Lake, from which (d)anglers pull up walleye, perch and bass.

Head to www.icefishing.org for full details on the Ice Fishing Extravaganza held each January.

9 Squid, Halong Bay, Vietnam

The word 'squid' mightn't conjure up the warm-and-fuzzies right now, but after a night on Halong Bay, that will change. Dozens of junks ply the bay's jade-green waters on moonless evenings, fishing for the slippery little cephalopods that go into the region's best-known speciality: squid sausages. With only a bamboo rod, a catch net and a lamp to attract the squid to the surface, anyone can hook themselves an impressive 30-plus squid in just a couple of hours. The stillness of the bay dotted by the dreamy reflection of the lamps makes for a contemplative, romantic evening.

Squid season in Halong begins in April and runs through until January: the biggest squid are caught between October and November.

10 Brown trout, Rio Grande, Tierra del Fuego

Tierra del Fuego is Spanish for 'Land of Fire', and au fait fly-fishers couldn't agree more: when it comes to trout, this place is *hot*. The archipelago boasts the world's best sea-run brown trout angling: the minimum average weight of the region's brown trout is 4kg (one in 50 catches are said to be 11kg or above), and the Rio Grande teems with an estimated 70,000 of the prized fish. Being at the end of the earth, Tierra del Fuego can be hard to get to, but Rio Grande's mammoth trout statue will let you know you've arrived.

Despite the abundance of trout, there are strict fishing restrictions on Tierra del Fuego: catch-and-release firmly applies. The fishing season is from December until mid-April.

● *By Tamara Sheward*

This aggressive predator has a history of attacking humans, and has been known to maul birds in flight

Top Travel Lists ●●●●●●● ●●●●●●

Wonders of the Small-Screen World

If you're not prone to television addiction and its consequent nerd-geek-fandom, look away now (try the list on p176 instead ...). Otherwise, prepare to make fiction come to life.

1 True Detective – *Vermillion Parish, South Louisiana, USA*

Immerse yourself in the mesmerising patchwork of flatland invaded by water, desolate roads of industrial obsolescence, and a dark history: *True Detective* swept through 2014's TV landscape like a rip tide. Beyond the horrors played out in the series, there's a rich and relatively unvisited part of the world to see: ecotourism, festivals, Cajun cuisine – all bathed in a special southern glow. To connect with your inner Rust Cohle try Palmetto Island State Park. A canoe trek through the ponds might give just a touch of that existential madness...

Visit palmettoisland.wordpress.com for more information on cabins and activities in the deep dark South.

2 Game of Thrones – *Northern Ireland, Iceland & Morocco*

It's dominated television viewing for a few years, why not put it on your travel itinerary? Northern Ireland is the series' home base and will give you plenty of fuel for your fantastical tourism dreams – try Tollymore State Forest where a number of outdoor scenes were filmed. But Iceland's Lake Mývatn provides the icy setting for the Night's Watch men, and the town of Ouarzazate on the edge of the desert in southern Morocco will bring the dragons to life as you relive the Khaleesi's trek with the Dothraki.

A number of driving routes are suggested at www.causewaycoastandglens.com/Game-of-Thrones-Itinerary.T1163.aspx.

3 Girls - *New York City, USA*

Hipster alert! But you knew that, so whatever, right? Lena Dunham's self-reflective, acerbic take on millennial coming-of-age trials and tribulations puts NYC back on the map (OK, it never left the map, but whatever). From Greenpoint's Café Grumpy where you'd find sanity in Ray, to the warehouses of Bushwick for the party scenes you're craving, it's Brooklyn, Williamsburg and the surrounds that'll give you a feel for the show. Expose your tattoos, cobble together a found-object outfit and hit the streets. You won't look back.

For your food, drink and partying needs while on the Girls *trail, try www.bushwickdaily.com.*

Expose your tattoos, cobble together a found-object outfit and hit the streets. You won't look back

4 Braquo - *Paris, France*

Not for the faint-hearted, *Braquo* is a dark, whirlwind car chase through the gritty streets (who knew?!) of Paris, where crime and violence are unexpectedly on tap. City of Light be damned! Head to Hauts-de-Seine, the inner-western suburbs of Paris, and wander around this off-the-tourist-trail area. But do it at night for the full, gloomy effect. The area is actually a wealthy one, and you needn't look past the gentile Parc de Saint Cloud for evidence, some 450 hectares of forests and gardens, and beautiful views of Paris.

La Défense is the cold corporate heart of Hauts-de-Seine, home to hotels, restaurants and a superb open-air museum on Parvis de la Défense.

Top Travel Lists

THE CITY OF PORTLAND MORE THAN LIVES UP TO THE HYPE OF COOLER-THAN-COOL TV SHOW *PORTLANDIA*

5 The Killing - *Copenhagen, Denmark*

First, visit the Pentecost Woods at Amager outside of Copenhagen, and witness the scene of the crime, the brutal murder that kicked off this chilling Danish crime series. Then back to the city, where you'll have to dodge the charm of the streets, the famous restaurants and the friendly people if you want to maintain a semblance of dark moodiness. Try a Peter and Ping Literary Walk for a guided view of Copenhagen through *The Killing* lens. *Peter and Ping also offer walks for other television shows, see them all at www.peter-og-ping.dk/default_uk.asp.*

6 Deadwood - *Deadwood, USA*

It's been a few years but the cussin' and fightin' of *Deadwood* still feels fresh – and a visit to the eponymous town in South Dakota will have you hankering for a whiskey before you can say '****sucker!' The show explored the origins of civilisations through the travails of a pioneering gold-digging community in the Black Hills, bringing America's violent and intrepid history into focus. You can relive it all here – a sign at 622 Main St announces the location of Wild Bill Hickok's shooting and a trip to Mount Moriah Cemetery will show some familiar names alongside Wild Bill, including Seth Bullock and Calamity Jane.

Get a glimpse into the pioneering life of a gold miner at Black Hills Mining Museum in nearby Lead (www.blackhillsminingmuseum.com).

7 Downton Abbey - *Hampshire, UK*

It may not be everyone's cup of tea, but it's hard to resist upstairs/downstairs machinations when they're so beautifully repressed and dressed. The focus is of course the stunning home to them all, Highclere Castle (aka Downton Abbey), and you can tour this stately abode and its surrounding gardens and woods at your leisure. Then it's off to Bampton, which plays the part of Downton itself. Visiting in spring means a chance to witness Morris Dancing Day. Unforgettable. *Don't miss the class-equalising dancing: www.traditionalbamptonmorris.org.uk.*

IT MAY LOOK LIKE SUBURBAN SPRAWL, BUT IS ALL AS IT SEEMS IN BREAKING BAD'S ALBUQUERQUE?

JOHN LUND © GETTY IMAGES

for a soy chamomile tea – you might want to hold the stevia though...

See www.lonelyplanet.com/usa/travel-tips-and-articles/a-do-it-yourself-breaking-bad-tour-of-albuquerque for a rundown on your options.

9 Sherlock – *London, UK*

Before the TV show, there was of course the book, and London has a rich Sherlock itinerary for those of us still not sure if he was actually real or not. The TV show has somehow made the story's fictitious nature more evident, but the sheer *fact* of London still makes it hard to let the belief go. So, with Sherlock as your guide... perhaps start at 187 North Gower St – the front door used as the entrance to Sherlock's abode, despite the actual address being 221B Baker St (where you'll find the Sherlock Homes Museum now). But for a true origin experience, visit St Bart's hospital, where Sherlock and Watson meet for the first time.

For a two-hour guided tour try www.britmovietours.com/bookings/sherlock-holmes-london-tour.

> **It may not be everyone's cup of tea, but it's hard to resist upstairs/downstairs machinations when they're so beautifully repressed and dressed**

8 Breaking Bad – *Albuquerque, USA*

It may be all over for Walt and Jesse, but the comic-like intensity of the series means it still echoes in the hearts and minds of fans with a vengeance. The meth-making and -selling high jinks and never-ending violence takes place in and around Albuquerque, New Mexico. Blue, blue skies, eternal deserts and empty suburban streets; the eerie calm of the location was a counterpoint to all the action. Relive scenes in Gus Fring's Pollos Hermanos (actually a burger and burrito restaurant called Twisters), or perhaps visit The Grove

10 Portlandia – *Portland, USA*

What do you do when a place becomes so cool, so ridiculously liveable, so eminently desirable, that lampooning it becomes a cult TV sensation? Well, you should probably just go there (pictured overleaf) anyway. When you're there you'll recognise the locales where Fred and Carrie carry out their brilliant satire of Portland hipster-middle-class life. But it won't faze you, instead the surrounding hiking and biking trails will beckon, the local produce and eating scene will inspire you and its famous craft brewing options will keep you refreshed.

www.travelportland.com/collection/portlandia provides an episode-by-episode overview of where fiction and reality meet on the streets of the city.

● *By Ben Handicott*

The Royal Wee: The World's Best Bathrooms

If you're curious about uncovering the world's best bathrooms then urine luck: these famous toilets are really making a splash.

1 Park Hyatt Tokyo, Japan

From singing johns to heated commodes, Japan has long been number one when it comes to number two. So where to begin in a land that has leapt so far forward in bathroom technology that the standard Western toilet seems archaic by comparison? It's best to stick with the classics, like Tokyo's first major luxury enclave, the sky-scraping Park Hyatt Tokyo, famous as the setting for Sofia Coppola's *Lost in Translation.* Hallways of signature Tiffany-esque blue lead to capacious suites that don't skimp on the swank. Expect robotic toilets covered in buttons and knobs that control everything from seat temperature to a bidet array. *Located close to the bustling Shinjuku station, the Park Hyatt Tokyo features two signature restaurants: kaiseki at Kozue and steaks at New York Grill.*

2 The Attendant, London, UK

Thomas Crapper pretty much sealed his fate when he became a plumber in London in the 19th century. Though not credited with the invention of the modern-day flusher, he did popularise the item and make several improvements. (Contrary to popular belief, the word 'crap' is from a Middle English term and not derived from his unfortunate name.) If you're seeking for the throwback charm of Crapper's London then look no further than the Attendant, a Victorian public toilet that has been cleverly transformed into one of the city's most talked-about cafes. Come for high tea and it'll be the most time you've ever spent in a WC. *Open from breakfast to afternoon tea, 8am–6pm Mon–Fri and 10am–5pm Sat; visit www.the-attendant.com.*

3 International Spacestation, Outer Space

The planet's most expensive toilet is really outta this world. Seriously. NASA owns the most costly crapper this side of the sun, reportedly a cool US$19 million to develop and construct. Take a pee at zero Gs and experience the genius design that compensates for the lack of gravity by employing an intricate system of air pumps, nozzles and levers to make sure the astronaut stays safely seated, and that all the waste remains in the bowl. Fun fact: the machine turns most of the liquid waste into potable water! *Sorry folks, you're going to need years of pilot training or a PhD in space sciences to try this one out, but after seeing Cuarón's* Gravity *we have a hunch that you're better off on dry land.*

4 Yangrenjie, Chongqing, China

Like some colossal shrine to bodily functions, the public restroom along the theme-park-y Yangrenjie, or 'Foreigner Street', in Chongqing, China, is in fact the largest in the world, with a whopping 1000 loos. A Pharaoh's face tops the pyramid of porcelain (your guess is as good as ours), and inside you'll find a 3200-sq-m maze of latrines in all sorts of strange designs. Make sure to scout out the toilets shaped like human legs or animal mouths for extra mirth.

Located in the Nan'an District of Chongqing; free of charge. Visit in daylight to enjoy the outdoor options.

5 Empire Hotel, Jerudong, Brunei

Imagine a zillion-tonne hunk of Italian marble dipped in gold and tossed into the rainforest – you've just pictured the Empire Hotel, a pet project of Brunei's prodigal Prince Jefri. With a construction budget around US$2 billion, the resort leaves nothing to be desired. Expect gilded fixtures, marble floors and an Emperor Suite with the world's most opulent private indoor swimming pool. Prices are kept astonishing low because – as popular rumour has it the hotel needs warm bodies to regularly flush the toilets and keep the massive plumbing system working. So do your civic duty and book a room for a few nights.

The hotel is located outside the capital city of Bandar Seri Begawan. See www.theempirehotel.com for more information.

THE UNDERWATER BATHROOMS AT ATLANTIS, THE PALM, DUBAI

Top Travel Lists

6 Centre Pompidou, Paris, France

Flip a urinal upside down, sign it with a fake name and voila: one of the world's most expensive pieces of art. Entitled *Fountain*, it was developed during the Dadaist era in New York City during the 1910s by Marcel Duchamp. Duchamp pioneered the popular anti-art movement, creating a series of 'ready-made' pieces out of pre-existing items like a bottle rack and a snow shovel. There are about 10 replicas of the work housed in several major art museums around the world including the esteemed Centre Pompidou in Paris. It is, without a doubt, the most photographed urinal in the world.
The museum is open from 11am to 9pm every day except Tuesday; it costs €13 to enter.

7 The Oberoi Amarvilas, Agra, India

Imagine overlooking one of the world's Seven Wonders from the privacy of your own bathroom. Agra's Oberoi Amarvilas takes guests on a sensorial journey back to an era of conquest and excess. It is well documented that the members of the Mughal elite enjoyed a luxurious lifestyle, with ample gardens, feasts, harems, sweeping palaces and many other ostentatious manifestations of wealth. So it's fitting that this luxury hotel pulls out all the stops including perfect views of the Taj Mahal from the bathroom of its Kohinoor suite. This throne is truly fit for royalty.
Agra is located about a four-hour drive from Delhi, and is best visited in the cooler months of December to March. See www.oberoihotels.com for more.

From singing johns to heated commodes, Japan has long been number one when it comes to number two

8 Ephesus, Selçuk, Turkey

The elaborate ruins of Ephesus offer insight into one of the most populated cities of the Roman Empire. Ephesus is the best-preserved classical city in the eastern Mediterranean, if not all of Europe, and was once the grand capital of the province of Asia, with over 250,000 inhabitants. Thousands of tourists ogle the towering Library of Celsus, but the most impressive feat is the system of piping for the so-called Terraced Houses. Covered in elaborate mosaics, the homes of Ephesus' wealthy elite offered one of the first examples of private bathrooms with flushing toilets – and that was over 2000 years ago.
The ruins of Ephesus are open daily from 8am to 6.30pm from May to Oct, and to 4.30pm from November to April. Admission is extra for the Terraced Houses portion of the site.

9 Atlantis, The Palm, Dubai

We all know it ends up in the ocean anyway, so why not go straight to the bottom line. At Atlantis, The Palm, you can use the john while surrounded by swimming fishes in the Poseidon or Neptune suites. Shell out some serious cash (no pun intended) to stay in one of the two submerged

IT'S LUXURY DRESSED UP, SAFARI-STYLE, AT MNEMBA ISLAND OFF THE COAST OF ZANZIBAR

rooms that offer views of over 65,000 marine creatures instead of the usual resort-y swaying palms and shimmering sand. Uniquely built with visiting dignitaries in mind, the suites puts a whole new meaning to the term 'royal flush'. *Day visits are available to the man-made islands off the coast of Dubai, but you'll have to book one of the exclusive suites for the full experience. Visit www.atlantisthepalm.com.*

Top Travel Lists

10 *Mnemba Island, Zanzibar, Tanzania*

Skip the glitz and the glam of solid gold toilets and other such distractions, and head out into nature itself when nature calls. Mnemba Island, a fringe reef island off the coast of Zanzibar, puts an elegant twist on the castaway vacation fantasy with its private cache of thatched *bandas;* simple huts abutting the curling tide. Open-air bathrooms perfectly mimic the back-to-the-wild experience, but everything's secretly luxe: hidden rain showers, designer products, butler attendants, and sweeping amounts of space. Robinson Crusoe never had it so good. *Rooms are US$1500 per person in high season and include full board and two scuba dives.*
● *By Brandon Presser*

Index

Index

Acknowledgements

*Published in October 2014
by Lonely Planet Publications Pty Ltd*

ABN 36 005 607 983

www.lonelyplanet.com

ISBN 978 1 74360 362 8

© Lonely Planet 2014

© Photographs as indicated 2014

Printed in Singapore

PUBLISHING DIRECTOR Piers Pickard
COMMISSIONING EDITOR AND PROJECT MANAGER Jessica Cole
COPYEDITOR Bridget Blair
ART DIRECTOR Dan Tucker
LAYOUT DESIGNER Austin Taylor
PRE-PRESS PRODUCTION Tag
PRINT PRODUCTION Larissa Frost

WRITTEN BY James Bainbridge, Sarah Baxter, Joe Bindloss, Abigail Blasi, Joshua Samuel Brown, Stuart Butler, Kerry Christiani, Fionn Davenport, Megan Eaves, Bridget Gleeson, Tom Hall, Ben Handicott, Anita Isalska, Virginia Jealous, Emily Matchar, Virginia Maxwell, Bradley Mayhew, Genevieve Paiement-Jacobson, Matt Phillips, Brandon Presser, Sarah Reid, Tim Richards, Tamara Sheward, Ryan Van Berkmoes, Tasmin Waby, Benedict Walker, Steve Waters, Luke Waterson, Cliff Wilkinson, Nicola Williams, Chris Zeiher
THANKS TO Alberto Capano, Jenni Davis, Emeline Gontier, Lou La Grange, Georgina Leslie, Anirban Mahapatra, Piers Pickard, Nùria Puig, Tom Spurling, Cliff Wilkinson

Lonely Planet offices

AUSTRALIA
90 Maribyrnong St, Footscray,
Victoria, 3011, Australia
Phone 03 8379 8000
Email talk2us@lonelyplanet.com.au

USA
150 Linden St, Oakland, CA 94607
Phone 510 250 6400
Email info@lonelyplanet.com

UNITED KINGDOM
Media Centre, 201 Wood Lane, London W12 7TQ
Phone 020 8433 1333
Email go@lonelyplanet.co.uk

Front cover image El Chalten and Mount Fitzroy, Argentina – Marion Faria Photography © Getty *Image captions* p2 western lowland gorilla, Republic of Congo, p6 Subotica, northern Serbia, p12 Medina of Fez, Morocco, p54 Gokyo Lake, Khumbu, p96 Piazza di Duomo, Milan, p204 Oryx, Gemsbok at Sossusvlei, Namibia, p207 Ometepe Island, Nicaragua, p208 Flores Island, Indonesia

Best in Travel starts with hundreds of ideas from everyone at Lonely Planet, including our extended family of travellers, bloggers and tweeters. Once we're confident we have the cream of 2015's travel choices, the final selection is made by a panel of in-house travel experts, based on topicality, excitement, value and that special X-factor. Our focus is on the merits of each destination and the unique experiences they offer travellers.

Although the authors and Lonely Planet have taken all reasonable care in preparing this book, we make no warranty about the accuracy or completeness of its content and, to the maximum extent permitted, disclaim all liability from its use.

Travel planner

Best in Travel 2015

BREELEY COOLE © GETTY IMAGES

January

Africa Cup of Nations, Morocco Africa's main soccer championship is hosted by Morocco this year, with matches set to fill stadiums in Tangier, Rabat, Marrakesh and Agadir from 17 January to 7 February. *Pages 50–53*

Ati-Atihan Festival, Kalibo, The Philippines Indigenous costumes with extravagant modern embellishments take centre-stage at this festival of dance, music and feasting from 17 to 19 January. *Pages 42–45*

Centenary Party, Rocky Mountain National Park, USA January 26 marks the 100th anniversary of President Woodrow Wilson's signing the bill that created the park. The event will be marked by a giant community birthday party. *Pages 60–63*

February

Sami Festival, Northern Norway In the eternal twilight of the Arctic midwinter, the Sami people host a week of traditional festivities in early February – the highlight is the reindeer-racing championships. *Pages 76–79*

Opera Ball, Vienna, Austria The Opera Ball (12 February) is the jewel in the crown of Vienna's 450 balls in January and February, where you can waltz, foxtrot and polonaise with the best. *Pages 126–129*

Sherpa New Year, Khumbu, Nepal Tibetan opera, masked dances and home-brewed *chang* (barley beer) add a buzz to the traditional new year festivities. *Pages 76–79*